Her Master

C000183583

in

Swaledale

a

Second Glance

Calver Hill and Healaugh.

Her Master's Walks
in
Swaledale
a
Second Glance

Stephen I. Robinson

BARLEY • PUBLISHING
2002

Barley Publishing
10 Mill Green View
Swarcliffe
Leeds LS14 5JT

www.hm-walks.co.uk
email: barley@hm-walks.co.uk

© S. I. Robinson 2002

ISBN 1 898550 03 4

Maps reproduced from Ordnance Survey mapping on behalf of
The Controller of Her Majesty's Stationery Office
© Crown Copyright. Licence Number MC100016545.

Drawings by Andrew Haddelsey
Maps and photographs by Stephen I. Robinson

All rights reserved.
No part of this publication may be reproduced,
stored in a retrieval system, or transmitted,
in any form or any means, electronic,
mechanical, photocopying, recording,
or otherwise, without the prior written
permission of the Copyright owner.

Printed in Great Britain by:
Impressions (Leeds) Limited
The Mint, Moor View, Leeds LS11 9NF
Telephone 0113 246 1075

Richmond Castle.

Contents

Paw-word by 'Her'

Having a book named after you is quite thrilling, *(and a whole series has been named after me)*. However, I have often thought the title should be 'Walks with Sherry and Him'. After all, I am the star of the books!

All the routes in these books have been walked personally by me, and it's a good job too! During one walk, I was following what my master would describe as 'an obvious path'. He stopped suddenly, and said, "Hold on Little Un, I think we have taken the wrong path." *(WE?! He's the one who drew the map.)* Anyhow we turned back and after a short distance he stopped again, saying, "It looks like we were on the right path after all." *(Told you it was an obvious path, didn't I?)*

Apart from his poor sense of direction my master's not so bad, although he does tease me sometimes. I can remember one walk, when a rabbit bolted across our path. Tauntingly he said, "Look Sherry, a rabbit, go get him, hee, hee." How could I? He

had hold of the lead! However, my luck was in, my master put his foot in one of the rabbits holes, fell over and dropped the lead. I was quick to chase the rabbit. It was fast. Too fast! It weaved in and out of the trees before vanishing down a hole. I began to dig and by the time my master caught up with me, the earth was flying in all directions. It was a hot day and the earth stuck to the sweat on his arms and face, he was a real filthy sight after that! *(Serves him right for teasing me, hee, hee!)*

I always enjoy walking, but my master seems to get tired long before I do! Could it be because he only has two legs?

Perhaps, Little Un, it's because I have to lift you over many of the stiles!

6

Introduction

I have developed a great affection for Swaledale over the years, its charm and serenity are difficult to beat. It embraces all the finest characteristics of the Dales landscape flaunting them with immense pride. Swaledale's reputation of being the most beautiful dale in Yorkshire is certainly well deserved.

Its river, the Swale, whose name means 'whirling, rushing river,' has wild origins on the High Seat ridge near the Cumbrian border. However, the actual birth of the river Swale takes place 2½ miles (4km) west of Keld. Here, two powerful mountain streams, Birkdale Beck and Great Sleddale Beck, merge to create the swiftest flowing river in England. It flows for 83 miles (133km) before joining with the river Ure at Myton-on-Swale, a few miles below Boroughbridge. According to Bede, St Paulinus, the first Archbishop of York, baptised 10,000 men and numerous women and children in this river in one day. This resulted in our Saxon ancestors referring to it as the Jordan of England.

Swaledale is the most northerly of the Yorkshire Dales and it is surrounded by some of the highest mountains of the Pennines; Lovely Seat, Great Shunner Fell, High Seat and Nine Standards Rigg, all towering to well over 2000 feet (630m). It has many tributary valleys, the largest being Arkengarthdale, often thought of as a separate dale. Arkengarthdale is a broad, remote valley which leaves Swaledale at Reeth and climbs north-west to the famous Tan Hill Inn. This is England's highest inn, standing at 1732 feet (528m) above sea level. It stands 4½ miles (7km) from Keld, the nearest village, surrounded by a bleak moorland wilderness.

The variety of wildlife habitats ranges from blanket bog and heather moorland to woodland and flower-rich hay meadows. Each provides a haven for birds, small mammals and wild flowers. The curlew, common sandpiper, dipper, grey and pied wagtail, snipe and oystercatcher are easy to spot. Stoats and weasels are often seen, hares are also quite common as is the occasional roe deer. Sightings of otters are rare but plans to reintroduce them into the river Swale are now under way. The hay meadows provide a spectacle of colour throughout the summer months, starting with yellow buttercups, followed by white pignut, blue cranesbill, ox-eye daisies and many other flowers.

This area is one of the most picturesque landscapes in England. Although the natural features were created millions of years ago by glacial erosion and weathering, man has also played a major part in its development. A succession of settlers have left their mark on this landscape; clearing woodland, building villages and roads, cultivating crops; and later building the field barns and dry stone walls which are such a distinctive feature of the area. The lead mining industry made a much harsher contribution to the landscape of Swaledale and Arkengarthdale, and the scars are visible during some of the walks.

Swaledale has a network of over 280 miles (450km) of public rights of way and both the 'Pennine Way' and the 'Coast-to-Coast Walk' pass through this beautiful dale. Its many attractive villages provide excellent starting places for a variety of walks from easy riverside rambles to more strenuous fell walks.

Whenever you choose to visit this area I am certain that it will be an enlightening experience for you to enjoy.

Stephen I. Robinson,

September 2002

Be Prepared!

Walking, arguably the most enjoyable of pastimes and undoubtedly one of the healthiest, can be tailored to meet the requirements of almost anyone.

Your preference might be for a gentle stroll of three to four miles along a quiet riverbank or woodland path, or perhaps a strenuous hill walk of ten miles or more. Whichever you choose, provided you are properly equipped, your walk will not only be safer but also more enjoyable. This does not mean taking everything including the kitchen sink! If you are a keen photographer a camera with spare films is essential. Binoculars are mandatory for birdwatchers. The artist needs his sketchbook and pencil. But remember, everything you take is extra weight to be carried.

What to wear and carry will depend on the season, the weather and good sense.

The items in the following lists are recommended, but think carefully about what to take. Some extra items may be needed on a hill walk which could be left behind when walking through the lower meadows. Due to our unpredictable climate, however, a spare wool sweater and waterproofs should always be carried. *(Items in italics could be used in warmer conditions.)*

TO WEAR

Strong walking boots or stout shoes
Thick woollen socks (two pairs)
Cotton shirt *or T-Shirt*
Walking breeches, trousers *or shorts*
(Never wear jeans, they lose their heat retention when wet.)
Woollen hat, balaclava *or sun hat*

TO CARRY

A small rucksack, thirty to forty litres in capacity, to carry the following:
Waterproof anorak or cagoule
Wool sweater or fibre pile jacket
Gloves, scarf
First aid kit, compass, whistle
Torch, pencil and note pad
Ordnance Survey map of the area
Emergency rations, survival bag
Water bottle with water
Food and snacks

OPTIONAL ITEMS

Camera and spare films, binoculars
Swiss army knife
Flask with tea, coffee, soup or other hot drink
Waterproof over-trousers, gaiters
Five to ten yards of thin cord
(Useful for temporary laces etc.)

Muker.

About the Walks

The routes chosen for this guide explore a variety of terrain and scenery. This includes swift flowing streams and spectacular waterfalls, heather-clad moorland and limestone scars, flower-rich hay meadows and woodland.

All of the walks follow circular routes ranging from 5½ to 9 miles (9 to 14.5km). They begin from a car park where one is available, or at a place where it is possible to park safely without causing obstruction.

Final surveys were carried out between March and August 2002. However, from time to time walls, fences and hedges may be removed, stiles and gates repositioned, buildings demolished and new forestry established. Therefore it is recommended that the relevant ordnance survey maps and a compass are carried. They will help to determine landmarks and where necessary alternative routes. Explorer OL30 covers all of the walks with the exception of walk 10 which requires Explorer 304.

Only the relevant area of the map has been used and then simplified so that only the walls, fences, buildings, rivers, roads and landmarks etc where the route passes through are included.

Each map has the route marked in red with numbered arrow pointers for each section of the route. These relate to the descriptive guide on the facing page, which includes a grid reference for each stage of the walk. When used together these features should help to avoid confusion, but common sense and some map reading experience are desirable.

The times given for completion of the walks are approximate and do not include any allowance for lunch breaks, photo stops or sightseeing. As a rule of thumb, adding one third of the stated time for stops should be sufficient. If accompanied by young children extra walking time will have to be allowed. Extended stays at any of the inns or tea shops *en route* should also be added to the time.

WHITSUNDALE and CLUMPSTONE HILL

from Keld 7½ miles (12km)

Some of Upper Swaledale's most spectacular scenery is revealed during this moderate hill walk. It follows a section of the 'Coast-to-Coast' footpath and the views are excellent throughout.

Our starting point is the charming village of Keld, the last settlement of any size in Swaledale. Its name comes from the Norse 'Kelda' which means spring or stream, but it was called Appeltrekelde until the late Middle Ages meaning 'the spring by the apple tree'. The Vikings certainly knew what they were doing when they settled at Keld. It is a perfect refuge, sheltered on all sides by rolling green hills. Nearby there are several waterfalls, including Catrake Force, East Gill Force, Wain Wath Force and the spectacular Kisdon Force.

Our route from Keld crosses the river Swale and climbs past the striking East Gill Force to arrive at East Stonesdale Farm. Two famous footpaths meet here; the Pennine Way heading north to Tan Hill and Scotland; and the Coast-to-Coast has reached its halfway point with 95 of its 190 miles completed.

The views from East Stonesdale are outstanding, with the High Seat ridge providing a magnificent backdrop. After passing the pretty Currack Force we continue above the limestone cliff of Cotterby Scar and into the peaceful valley of Whitsundale. The path takes us past the dramatic gorge of Oven Mouth, whose steep crags and sharp cleft provide fine views of Whitsundale Beck. Further on, we pass the narrow gorge at How Edge Scars where a waterfall plunges steeply through the trees into the beck below. Approaching Ravenseat another attractive waterfall is revealed.

Ravenseat is Swaledale's remotest settlement, situated on the old jagger road to Tan Hill and Teesdale. Eleven families once lived here. Most of the men worked in the coal mines at Tan Hill and had to travel the jagger road twice each day in all weathers, often soaked and chilled to the bone. It has an ancient packhorse bridge with a high humpback and its original stone cobbled surface remains. The term 'jagger' was applied to the man in charge of a packhorse train. It derived from the German 'Jaeger' pony, one of the hardy packhorse breeds commonly used in the Dales. Packhorse trains consisted of between twenty and forty ponies, in the charge of a driver and one or two helpers. The leading pony had a bell, to warn travellers and other packhorse trains of their approach, so that a passing place could be found.

From Ravenseat we follow the road to Black Howe, where we descend through the fields to Hoggarth Bridge. During the descent the large farmhouse of Hoggarths can be seen to the right. It was rebuilt on this site after the first house had been washed away by flood in 1899. In that year a cloudburst on Great Shunner Fell caused large volumes of water to rush down Great Ash Gill behind Hoggarths, which at that time was situated lower down, on the south side of the river Swale. The people in the farmhouse had just enough time to escape through a bedroom window, but when the floodwaters subsided the house was little more than a ruin.

Leaving Hoggarth Bridge we climb over Clumpstone Hill and drop gently down into Angram. During the early nineteenth century, an evening school was held in one of Angram's cottages. The teacher had to give his lessons with chalk on the flags of the kitchen floor. His pupils, all past childhood, travelled many miles for their 'bit of learning'. This education was not free, each pupil had to pay a small sum to the teacher.

The road could be followed back to Keld, but our route favours the little valley of Skeb Skeugh Beck. The river Swale flowed through this valley until the end of the last Ice Age. Debris left behind by the melting glacier formed a dam across the valley. The river created a new route, cutting the deep gorge on the eastern side of Kisdon, forming the isolated hill we see today.

After crossing the valley we join the Pennine Way footpath which leads back into the village square at Keld.

Start/Parking:	Keld, there is a good sized car park at Park Lodge Farm just off the village square.
Location:	Keld is situated on the B6270 Richmond to Kirby Stephen road 23 miles (37km) west of Richmond.
Grid Ref:	893 012.
Distance:	7½ miles (12km) circular. Allow 4 to 4½ hrs.
OS Maps:	Explorer OL30 (1:25,000) or Landranger 91 (1:50,000).
Refreshments:	Park Lodge Farmhouse at Keld.
Public Toilets:	Keld, between the road junction and the village square.
Other:	The United Reform Church, youth hostel, telephone, bus service.

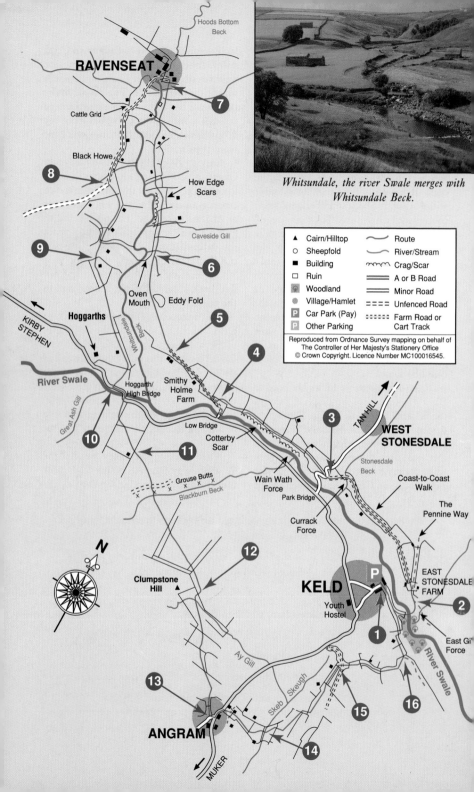

Whitsundale, the river Swale merges with Whitsundale Beck.

Hoods Bottom Beck

RAVENSEAT

⑦

Cattle Grid

Black Howe

⑧

How Edge Scars

Caveside Gill

⑨

⑥

Oven Mouth

Eddy Fold

Hoggarths

⑤

KIRBY STEPHEN

Whitsundale Beck

④

Smithy Holme Farm

③

TAN HILL

WEST STONESDALE

River Swale

Hoggarth/ High Bridge

Low Bridge

Cotterby Scar

Stonesdale Beck

Great Ash Gill

⑩

⑪

Wain Wath Force

Park Bridge

Coast-to-Coast Walk

The Pennine Way

Grouse Butts

Blackburn Beck

Currack Force

EAST STONESDALE FARM

⑫

Clumpstone Hill

KELD

②

N

⑬

ANGRAM

Ay Gill

Skeb Skeugh

Youth Hostel

①

East Gill Force

⑯

⑮

⑭

MUKER

Legend

▲ Cairn/Hilltop
○ Sheepfold
■ Building
□ Ruin
🌲 Woodland
● Village/Hamlet
🅿 Car Park (Pay)
🅿 Other Parking

〜 Route
〜 River/Stream
〜〜 Crag/Scar
═══ A or B Road
━━━ Minor Road
==== Unfenced Road
····· Farm Road or Cart Track

Reproduced from Ordnance Survey mapping on behalf of The Controller of Her Majesty's Stationery Office © Crown Copyright. Licence Number MC100016545.

✓ D. not good (-Bogs)

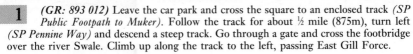

1   Whitsundale and Clumpstone Hill

1 *(GR: 893 012)* Leave the car park and cross the square to an enclosed track *(SP Public Footpath to Muker)*. Follow the track for about ½ mile (875m), turn left *(SP Pennine Way)* and descend a steep track. Go through a gate and cross the footbridge over the river Swale. Climb up along the track to the left, passing East Gill Force.

2 *(GR: 896 011)* At a junction of tracks *(PW and C to C)* take the left track climbing to East Stonesdale Farm. Take the left fork through the farmyard and follow the farm lane which leads to the road above Park Bridge.

3 *(GR: 887 016)* Cross the road, climb uphill for a few yards and go through the gate on the left, just above the bend *(SP Footpath)*. Follow the right wall and go through a gate. Now continue with the left boundary along the top of Cotterby Scar.

4 *(GR: 877 016)* Pass through a gap in the left wall, turn right and follow a rough farm track. Keep right at a fork and continue past Smithy Holme via two gates.

5 *(GR: 873 018)* When the track fades out near a barn, head right towards a signpost on the hillside above *(Ravenseat ¾ - Keld 1¾)*. Continue along a boggy path passing below a large sheepfold *(Eddy Fold)*, to Oven Mouth.

6 *(GR: 869 022)* Follow the left boundary through three fields. After passing the How Edge Scars continue straight ahead, keeping to the higher ground and to the right of a barn. Pass to the left of two barns in the next pasture *(Ravenseat comes into view)*. Continue via a gate and two gap stiles to enter the hamlet.

7 *(GR: 863 033)* Turn left and follow the farm lane down to cross the packhorse bridge. Continue along a tarmac road, over a cattle grid and past Black Howe.

8 *(GR: 863 025)* Turn left *(SP Footpath to Hoggarth Bridge)* cross a ladder stile and follow the left wall past two barns. Go through a gap stile, descend through a broken wall and climb back up keeping to the right of a barn.

9 *(GR: 865 020)* Go through a gap stile to the left of the gate. Follow the right wall and begin to descend via four more gap stiles to the road near Hoggarth Bridge. *(Hoggarth Bridge is also shown on some maps as High Bridge.)*

10 *(GR: 870 014)* Turn left and cross the bridge. Leave the road via a gate opposite *(SP Angram 1½ m)* and climb the steep bank to a ladder stile. Cross the stile and climb diagonally across two fields via two more ladder stiles.

11 *(GR: 874 011)* Continue across open moorland and descend to Blackburn Beck. Cross the beck near a line of grouse butts. Keep to the same heading and climb back up to pass through a step/gap stile combination. Cross a large pasture to another step/gap stile combination. Continue along a narrow path close to the wall.

12 *(GR: 883 004)* Go through a stile on the right and cross a stream. Climb to the far wall corner, bear half right and go through a gap stile. Cross a small hollow to another gap stile and follow the left wall to a gate. Descend via two gates to Angram.

13 *(GR: 888 997)* Turn left and continue to the main road, turn left and after about 50 yards (46m) leave the road via a gate on the right. Descend to a barn and pass through a gap to the right of it. Continue descending and go through an open gateway and bear left to cross Skeb Skeugh Beck via a bridge in the bottom corner.

14 *(GR: 891 999)* Head half left and go through a gap stile, climb steeply to a stile in the left corner of the field. Turn right and climb to a stile in the top wall. Turn left and follow the wall through two gates.

15 *(GR: 894 005)* Cross a broad stone track and climb up to a gate on the left. Go through the gate and follow a clear path over the hillside.

16 *(GR: 897 008)* Go through a gated stile on the left, continue to the right of a barn. Pass through a gate onto a broad track, turn left and go through a gate. Follow a clear enclosed track leading back to village square at Keld.

A CIRCUIT OF
KISDON ISLAND

from Keld 5½ miles (9km)

This wonderful walk circles the heather-clad limestone mass of Kisdon Hill. It has a good variety of terrain and scenery. The views are excellent and will certainly be memorable.

Keld is surrounded by some of the wildest countryside in Yorkshire. Nine Standards Rigg, Great Shunner Fell, Lovely Seat, and Rogan's Seat are among the outstanding features. It is a sedate little village, with its collection of cottages huddled around a small open square.

People living in such wild places need to be sturdy and strong minded. This was demonstrated in 1789 when Edward Stillman became pastor of a ruined chapel at Keld. Needing funds for repairs, he embarked on a remarkable walk to London and back, raising £700 from preaching and

begging. Another tribute to Edward Stillman's character lies in the fact that his total expenses for the journey came to only sixpence. After rebuilding the chapel he served the people of Keld for forty-eight years. The chapel was rebuilt again in 1860 with the added features of a bell and a sundial. Near the road junction at the top of the village is the former Cat Hole Inn. This became a private house in 1954, and now serves only diesel from a solitary pump.

From Keld we follow the road down the valley for a short distance where a stile leads onto a meadow path below Angram. Across the valley of Skeb Skeugh Beck is the heather clad Kisdon Hill. This shapely hill, encircled with limestone scars, reaches a mere 1636 feet (499m), but it still gives access to some of the finest views in Upper

Swaledale. It was formed during the last Ice Age, when glacial action widened the valleys and smoothed the hill tops. As the glacier retreated a debris of rocks and boulder clay blocked the valley, diverting the river Swale to its present course, leaving Kisdon as an isolated hill. On Jeffrey's Map of Yorkshire, 1771, it is shown as 'Kisdon Island'.

During our descent to Thwaite, the views are impressive. Lovely Seat directly ahead remains prominent throughout.

Thwaite is a welcome oasis for many thousands of Pennine Way walkers as they descend from the heights of Great Shunner Fell. It is a picturesque village with a small humpback bridge spanning a turbulent tributary of the river Swale. In 1899, a great storm drenched the dale and the normally placid Thwaite Beck became a raging torrent. Dogs, sheep, hen-houses and roofs were swept away by the force of the water. The cottage gardens near the beck were also engulfed by the deluge. It was said 'the flowers planted at Thwaite bloomed the next year at Muker', 2 miles (3km) away!

The village was the birthplace of two famous brothers, Richard and Cherry Kearton. They were pioneers in wildlife photography from the 1890s well into the twentieth century. The cottage in which they lived is marked by a stone lintel carved with animals and birds. The Kearton's used many ingenious methods to get closer to their subjects including a papier mâché cow, which tended to blow over in strong winds and apparently it once encouraged the attentions of a bull!

Leaving Thwaite we follow the Pennine Way, climbing steeply to Kisdon Farm. Below is the attractive village of Muker with the river Swale disappearing into the distance. Great Shunner Fell, the Buttertubs Pass and Lovely Seat complete the panorama. Our route continues along the Pennine Way, traversing the higher slopes of Kisdon Hill. Across the valley there are excellent views of Ivelet Moor, Swinner Gill and the forlorn ruins of Crackpot Hall.

Less than a mile from the finish of our walk, we should, if time allows, make a detour to visit the spectacular Kisdon Force. This has the reputation of being Swaledale's finest waterfall. Here the river Swale plunges 30 feet (10m) over two cascades. It tumbles down a small upper fall into a beautiful tree shaded pool, taking an encore over the lower fall. The area near the falls is often wet and slippery so extra care should be taken.

From the falls we retrace our steps and continue along the Pennine Way path returning to Keld.

Start/Parking:	Keld, there is a good sized car park at Park Lodge Farm just off the village square.
Location:	Keld is situated on the B6270 Richmond to Kirby Stephen road 23 miles (37km) west of Richmond.
Grid Ref:	893 012.
Distance:	5½ miles (9km) circular. Allow 2¾ hrs plus an extra 30 mins if you wish to visit Kisdon Force.
OS Maps:	Explorer OL30 (1:25,000) or Landranger 91 (1:50,000).
Refreshments:	Park Lodge Farmhouse at Keld, the Kearton Guest House at Thwaite.
Public Toilets:	Keld, between the road junction and the village square.
Other:	The United Reform Church, youth hostel, bus service, telephone.

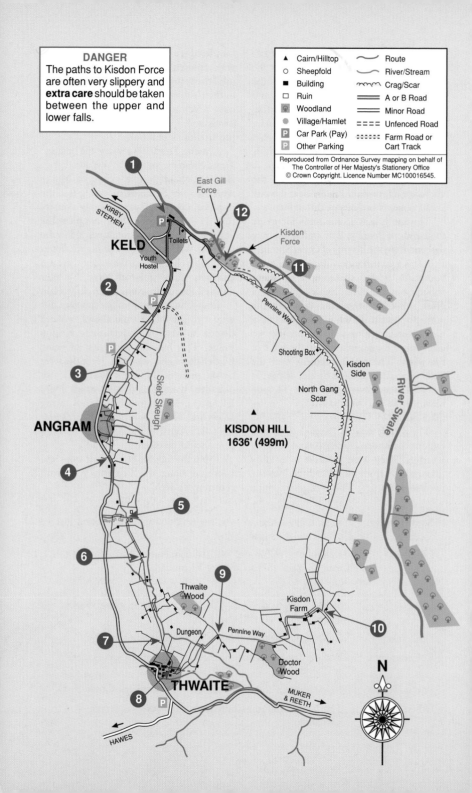

DANGER
The paths to Kisdon Force are often very slippery and **extra care** should be taken between the upper and lower falls.

Legend:
- ▲ Cairn/Hilltop
- ○ Sheepfold
- ■ Building
- □ Ruin
- 🌲 Woodland
- 🔴 Village/Hamlet
- 🅿 Car Park (Pay)
- 🅿 Other Parking
- ～ Route
- ～ River/Stream
- ⌒⌒⌒ Crag/Scar
- ═══ A or B Road
- ═══ Minor Road
- ==== Unfenced Road
- ⋯⋯⋯ Farm Road or Cart Track

Reproduced from Ordnance Survey mapping on behalf of The Controller of Her Majesty's Stationery Office © Crown Copyright. Licence Number MC100016545.

East Gill Force

KIRBY STEPHEN

KELD

Toilets

Youth Hostel

Kisdon Force

Pennine Way

Shooting Box

Kisdon Side

North Gang Scar

River Swale

Skeb Skeugh

ANGRAM

KISDON HILL
1636' (499m)

Skeb Gill

Thwaite Wood

Kisdon Farm

Dungeon

Pennine Way

Doctor Wood

THWAITE

HAWES

MUKER & REETH

N

2 A Circuit of Kisdon Island

1 *(GR: 893 012)* Leave the car park, turn right and follow the road to the junction by the telephone box at the top of the village. Turn left and continue along the road towards Muker and Thwaite.

2 *(GR: 892 005)* After about ½ mile *(0.8km)*, go through a gated stile on the left *(SP Thwaite)*. Bear right and go over another stile *(SP Footpath)*, continue ahead on a waymarked path through four gap stiles *(watch your head at the 3rd stile especially if you are over 5 feet (1.5m) in height)*, to reach a wooden footbridge at Ay Gill.

3 *(GR: 890 002)* Cross the bridge, climb a few steps and continue on a more obvious route through the pastures, passing below Angram, to the main road.

4 *(GR: 889 996)* Turn left and follow the road between two barns. About 50 yards *(46m)* past the barns leave the road through a gated stile on the left *(SP Footpath)*, bear right and begin descending to Thwaite. Pass to the left of a barn and go through a stile near the corner of the wall. Continue descending and cross a stream.

5 *(GR: 890 992)* Follow a faint track and pass through a gated stile behind a tree. Turn left and keeping to the wall side go through two gated stiles to reach a barn.

6 *(GR: 891 989)* Go through a gated stile *(watch your head, another stile with height restrictions)*, continue through three gap stiles and then follow the beck downstream. Leave the beckside and follow a flagged path to go through a gap stile in the wall corner.

7 *(GR: 892 984)* Head diagonally across the next field and go through a gap stile, bear half left and go through another gap stile. Bear right and follow a farm lane past the barns and go through a gap stile onto a narrow lane.

8 *(GR: 893 982)* *(Thwaite village can be visited via a gap stile to the right).* Turn left and follow the lane through two gap stiles. Turn left and pass through a gate, continue across the meadow, cross a bridge and go through a gate. Head to the right wall and climb up steeply to a gap stile in the top right corner.

9 *(GR: 896 984)* Turn right and follow a narrow track climbing gradually through the heather. Go through a gap stile, follow the left wall and go through a gate. Now follow the right wall, turn right at the wall corner and continue to Kisdon Farm. Continue through two gates and along a walled lane to a junction. Turn right *(SP Pennine Way)* and descend a short distance.

10 *(GR: 904 986)* Turn left *(SP Pennine Way)*, Climb up a broad track, leading over a wooden stile and a ladder stile. The path levels out and is very easy to follow along the shoulder of Kisdon Hill.

11 *(GR: 899 007)* Turn right *(SP Pennine Way)*, through the wall and descend to a junction. Take the left track *(SP Pennine Way)* and continue descending.

12 *(GR: 896 009)* Turn right *(SP Kisdon Upper Falls)* and follow a narrow track to visit Kisdon Force. Retrace steps to point 12, continue along the track and go through a gate. This track leads back to the village square at Keld.

NEDDY DICK - THE WORLDS FIRST ROCK STAR!

In the 1890s Richard Alderson, known locally as 'Neddy Dick', was climbing near Kisdon Force when he dislodged a rock. This struck another rock with a musical sound. Realising different stones produced different notes of music, he scoured the bed of the river Swale for other melodious stones, eventually creating his own 'heavy rock band' which he played with two wooden sticks. Neddy was encouraged by the local community and even made plans for a tour of the country. Sadly, he died just a few days before his debut.

IVELET MOOR and SWINNER GILL

from Gunnerside 9 miles (14.5km)

Heather-clad moors, fine views and the remains of the lead mining industry are the main features of this superb walk. It starts from Gunnerside, once described as 'The Klondyke of the Dale'.

This title came about because of its wealthy lead mining industry. The most active period was between 1780 and 1820, but large quantities of lead were mined until the 1880s. The decline of the lead mining industry was caused by; more costly lead extraction due to gradual vein exhaustion; cheap imports of lead from abroad. By the end of the nineteenth century most of the mines had closed. The miners left to seek work farther afield in the coal mines of Durham and Lancashire. Work there was plentiful and well paid when compared to the meagre earnings they had received whilst working in the lead mines of Swaledale.

Religion played an important role in the miners' lives, donations from their hard earned wages helped to build the large Methodist chapel below the bridge. It was originally built in 1789 at a cost of £600, making it one of Swaledale's earliest Wesleyan chapels. The miners did most of the preliminary building work such as the quarrying of stone and cutting the foundations. Methodism was also favoured by the mine owners, who approved of any belief which preached the virtues of hard work and sobriety.

From Gunnerside we follow a beautiful meadow path to the sleepy hamlet of Ivelet, most famous for its picturesque packhorse bridge. On the north side of the bridge, set into the verge, is a 'coffin stone', where

18

pall bearers rested their burden during their journey along the 'Corpse Road' from Keld to Grinton. Until the church at Muker was built in 1580, the nearest consecrated ground was at St Andrew's in Grinton. The corpse was carried in a wicker basket, by relays of bearers from villages along the way. The 12 mile (19km) journey from Keld often took two days.

Leaving the bridge we climb up through meadows to Calvert Houses and join a tarmac lane. Here there are exceptional views of Muker Side, Kisdon Hill and Great Shunner Fell. At the end of the lane a rough track leads to the river Swale which is followed upstream to Swinner Gill.

As we pass through Swinner Gill its stark beauty reveals a deep ravine, several striking waterfalls and a well preserved stone bridge. Above the bridge is an area known as Swinnergill Kirk. This was a meeting place for Nonconformist worship during the days of religious persecution. A look-out was placed on the fell above where he could watch the approaches. If a warning was given the service ended and the people in the congregation took shelter in a cave beside the falls.

Our walk continues uphill to the open moorland where magnificent panoramic views unfold. On a clear day the distant fells of Ribblesdale and Wharfedale are visible. To the right of the track, near the highest point, is Moss Dam, a former water source for the mines.

Continuing along the Coast-to-Coast footpath we descend into the great canyon of Gunnerside Gill. After passing through large areas of mining debris we reach the Blakethwaite smelt mill and peat store.

The smelt mill was built in 1820 to process ore from the rich Blakethwaite vein. It had twin ore furnaces separated by a wall. The wall and the four cast iron pillars would have supported the three arches that made up the front of each furnace. Behind the furnaces was the water-wheel and the bellows, and behind them, a roasting hearth. The course of the flue, climbing 150 feet (46m) up the hillside, can be traced, but the terminating chimney has gone. Sited high on the crag above the mill is a limekiln where limestone was burnt on the spot for building use. The building across the beck with the four wide arches was the peat store. This held enough fuel for a full year's smelting.

From Blakethwaite a broad green path leads up the hillside to Botcher Gill. Here we join a stony track and begin a gradual descent along Gunnerside Gill. The dramatic scenery of the gill and the surrounding hills can be appreciated all the way back to Gunnerside.

Start/Parking:	Gunnerside, parking is available in the village square near the literary institute or near the river bridge.
Location:	Gunnerside is situated on the B6270 Richmond to Kirby Stephen road 17 miles (27km) west of Richmond.
Grid Ref:	951 982.
Distance:	9 miles (14.5km) circular. Allow 5 hrs.
OS Maps:	Explorer OL30 (1:25,000) or Landranger 98 and 92 (1:50,000).
Refreshments:	The King's Head Inn, the Ghyllfoot Tea Rooms.
Public Toilets:	Gunnerside, by the side of the King's Head Inn.
Other:	Post Office, Methodist chapel, literary institute, telephone, bus service.

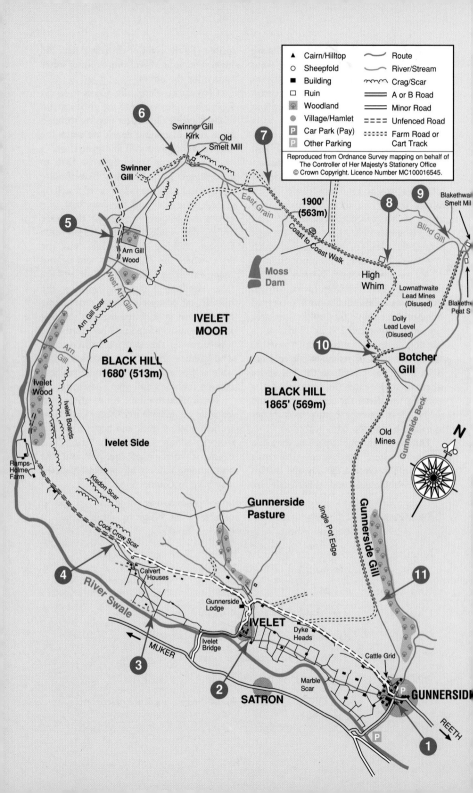

3 Ivelet Moor and Swinner Gill

1 *(GR: 951 982)* From the car park pass in front of East View Cottage and turn right, this road leads past the village school and through a gate on the right between the Flatlands housing area *(SP to Ivelet)*. Pass through four fields. At the fifth field, ignore the stile to the left and continue along the fence going through a further nine gap stiles, keeping roughly at the same level.

2 *(GR: 937 980)* Cross the beck via the footbridge and continue into Ivelet Village. Turn left at the road and follow it downhill to Ivelet Bridge. Go through a gate to the right of the bridge *(SP footpath Muker)* and continue on a clear route crossing two meadows.

3 *(GR: 929 978)* Bear half right and climb up through a gate in a fence and then continue to the top corner of the field. Go through a gap stile, turn left and proceed through two gap stiles into Calvert Houses. Turn right and leave the farmyard, follow a faint track which leads up onto a tarmac road.

4 *(GR: 923 981)* Turn left and follow the road passing above Rampsholme Farm. When the tarmac ends continue on a rough track descending to the riverside. Follow the river upstream to Arn Gill Wood.

5 *(GR: 910 004)* Cross a step stile and continue across the corner to cross another step stile. Climb up the steep slope and cross Swinner Gill.

6 *(GR: 912 012)* Turn right and follow a broad track over a stone bridge *(this is the Coast-to-Coast footpath)*. Continue on a narrow path climbing steadily uphill out of the valley. Cross a broad stone track *(SP footpath)* and proceed across a boggy section to rejoin the stone track higher up.

7 *(GR: 929 014)* Turn right and follow the stone track, go through a gate and continue past a line of grouse butts.

8 *(GR: 932 013)* Turn left at a sheepfold, leaving the track to follow a cairned path. The path descends gradually at first, then more steeply near Blind Gill.

9 *(GR: 936 018)* Turn right onto a narrow track doubling back and descending into Gunnerside Gill. At the bottom turn left onto a broad green track and follow it down to the Blakethwaite smelt mill and peat store. After exploring the ruins climb back up the green track and continue uphill to Botcher Gill.

10 *(GR: 935 002)* Turn left and join a broad track, continue over a bridge and go through a gate. Now begin a gradual descent along Gunnerside Gill.

11 *(GR: 946 987)* Turn left *(marked by a small cairn)*, leaving the broad track to descend steeply towards Gunnerside. Near some hawthorn trees bear slightly right and then follow the path down through a depression. Head to the left of the cottages to go through a gated stile. Keep close to the left fence and descend to the car park.

IVELET'S HAUNTED BRIDGE!

The packhorse bridge at Ivelet, which has an attractive single-spanned high stone arch, was built about 1695. The area around the bridge is so quiet that it is easy to imagine the packhorses laden with their heavy panniers crossing over the bridge and plodding their way along the peaceful tree-shaded lane. According to local folklore, the area around this ancient bridge is haunted by a headless dog which brings bad luck to anyone who sees it. The dog is usually sighted gliding onto the bridge, where it disappears over the edge.

4

QUIET-BULL
KEEP GATE
CLOSED!

SMARBER, BLADES and KEARTON

from Gunnerside 8 miles (13km)

This invigorating ramble visits some of Swaledale's hidden hamlets. The riverside return is delightful and has a good selection of birds and wild flowers to enjoy.

Gunnerside was originally two smaller settlements, Lodge Green on the east side of the beck and Gunnerside on the west. It now incorporates both and is a sizeable village. Closer inspection of the well kept cottages will reveal that many of them are made up of two, or sometimes three, smaller dwellings. These were built to house the lead miners in the eighteenth century and offered very scanty accommodation.

The literary institute, now serving as the village hall, was built in 1877 at a cost of £400. It had a smoking-room, reading-room, lecture hall and library, containing some 400 volumes. The building of these

small literary institutes and libraries in many of the villages, was the result of a desire for learning and self-improvement by the poorer members of the community. Most evenings they were packed with men learning to read and write. They were also used as public meeting places for lectures and for entertainment. Concerts were held and 'penny readings' helped to relieve the monotony of village life.

Leaving the village we follow part of the old Corpse Road climbing steeply up the hillside. As height is gained there is a wonderful view of Gunnerside Bottoms. The patchwork of walls and field barns are relics of the sixteenth century. Our route continues through Great Rowleth Wood, a haven for wild flowers, with bluebells, primroses and violets forming a carpet of colour in the open glades. The wood is mainly ash, elm and sycamore and among the bird life are blackcap, song thrush, and willow warbler.

From the wood we continue through the fields to Smarber. It was here in 1690 that Philip, Lord Wharton, a staunch advocate of the Puritan cause and friend of Oliver Cromwell, built Swaledale's first Independent chapel for Nonconformist worship. At that time chapels could not be built within 5 miles (8km) of any Anglican church; Smarber is just outside that limit from St Andrew's at Grinton. In 1692, Wharton founded a charity to distribute Bibles to children who could recite seven specified psalms by heart. In his youth, Wharton enjoyed a reputation as the handsomest young man in England. He was an enthusiastic dancer, an exercise in which he could show off his fine legs.

After passing through Smarber, a broad track is followed uphill onto a tarmac lane. It leads to the hamlet of Blades, high on the hillside. It was here where Methodism first took root in the dale. Soon after the first visit of John Wesley in 1761, William Spensley of Blades prepared a cottage adjoining his house for divine worship. Wesley always stayed with the Spensleys when he visited Swaledale.

The lane is actually a continuation of the Corpse Road and a little further on, at Riddings Farm, in the corner of a meadow, are the remains of a barn known as the 'Dead House'. Funeral processions on their way to Grinton are said to have stopped here for the night. The bearers would leave the wicker coffin in the Dead House while they went down to the Punch Bowl Inn at Feetham for refreshments!

When the road descends to Feetham, we continue along a walled track and after crossing the road, from Arkengarthdale to Feetham, another track leads to Kearton. The origin of the name is uncertain but possibly means 'farmstead belonging to Kærir'. To the east lies Park Hall and Healaugh Park a large house and estate once owned by the Whartons.

From Kearton we descend steeply through the fields to the main road. After a few hundred yards we leave the road and pass through Feetham Wood to reach the banks of the river Swale. From here our route follows the river upstream returning to Gunnerside.

The spectacular scenery is enriched with a wide variety of birds attracted by the river. Species to look out for include; dipper, oystercatcher, pied and yellow wagtails, redshank and sand martin. The area is also well known for its abundance of wild flowers including; meadowsweet, cowslip, primrose and red campion.

Start/Parking:	Gunnerside, parking is available in the village square near the literary institute or near the river bridge.
Location:	Gunnerside is situated on the B6270 Richmond to Kirby Stephen road 17 miles (27km) west of Richmond.
Grid Ref:	951 982.
Distance:	8 miles (13km) circular. Allow 4 hrs.
OS Maps:	Explorer OL30 (1:25,000) or Landranger 98 (1:50,000).
Refreshments:	The King's Head Inn and the Ghyllfoot Tea Rooms.
Public Toilets:	Gunnerside, by the side of the King's Head Inn.
Other:	Post Office, Methodist chapel, literary institute, telephone, bus service.

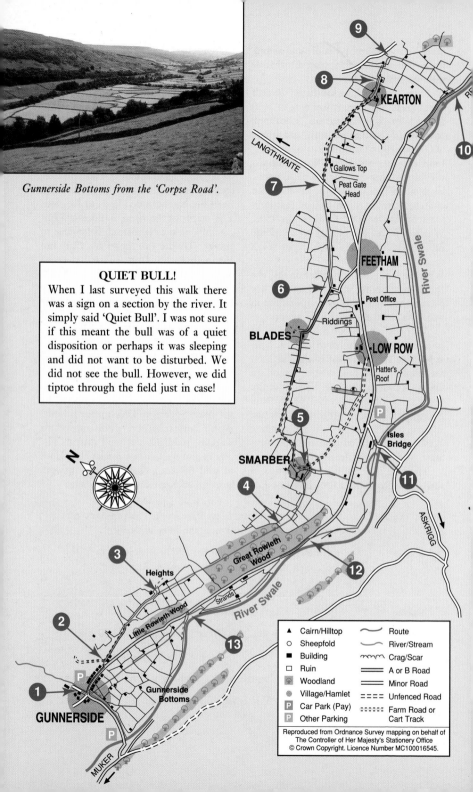

Gunnerside Bottoms from the 'Corpse Road'.

QUIET BULL!
When I last surveyed this walk there was a sign on a section by the river. It simply said 'Quiet Bull'. I was not sure if this meant the bull was of a quiet disposition or perhaps it was sleeping and did not want to be disturbed. We did not see the bull. However, we did tiptoe through the field just in case!

KEARTON

LANGTHWAITE

Gallows Top

Peat Gate Head

FEETHAM

River Swale

Post Office

Riddings

BLADES

LOW ROW

Hatter's Roof

SMARBER

Isles Bridge

ASKRIGG

Great Rowleth Wood

Heights

Little Rowleth Wood

Strands

River Swale

Gunnerside Bottoms

GUNNERSIDE

MUKER

Symbol	Legend	Symbol	Legend
▲	Cairn/Hilltop		Route
○	Sheepfold		River/Stream
■	Building		Crag/Scar
□	Ruin		A or B Road
	Woodland		Minor Road
P	Car Park (Pay)	====	Unfenced Road
P	Other Parking	······	Farm Road or Cart Track

Reproduced from Ordnance Survey mapping on behalf of The Controller of Her Majesty's Stationery Office © Crown Copyright. Licence Number MC100016545.

4 Smarber, Blades and Kearton

1 *(GR: 951 982)* From the car park, cross the bridge and follow the road past the King's Head Inn.

2 *(GR: 954 982)* Leave the main road, go through a gate and follow a tarmac lane to a left bend. At the bend leave the lane and continue straight ahead on an enclosed stone track. After crossing a beck the track becomes greener and leads uphill to Heights.

3 *(GR: 959 982)* Cross a stone step stile and pass below the farmhouse. Continue through four gap stiles and enter Great Rowleth Wood. Follow a clear path through the wood.

4 *(GR: 969 977)* From the wood go directly across the field and pass through an open gateway, bear left and climb up through two gap stiles. Continue beside the left wall passing through a gate to reach Smarber. At the farm turn right and follow a farm track through a gate and over a stream.

5 *(GR: 973 978)* Turn left and follow a broad track uphill. Remain on the track when it changes to a concrete surface. After reaching the open moor turn right and the track changes again to a tarmac surface. Follow this to pass through the tiny hamlet of Blades where the road begins to descend more steeply.

6 *(GR: 984 984)* At a sharp right hand bend *(near Brocca Cottage/East Brocca Bank)* turn left and leave the road. Continue along an enclosed green track passing through one gate returning to the open moor. Follow the right wall and when the track becomes stonier continue along it to the road.

7 *(GR: 990 989)* Cross the road and follow a farm track *(SP Kearton ½)*. At Gallows Top leave the track temporarily and follow the right wall. After rejoining the track continue through a gate into Kearton, keep left passing above the main farm buildings.

8 *(GR: 998 990)* Pass behind the cottage and go through a gated stile to the left of the barn. Turn right and follow the wall. Go through a gap stile, turn right and cross a large wooden step stile. Turn left and climb up to a gap stile in the top right corner.

9 *(GR: 000 990)* Turn right *(SP Footpath)* and follow the right wall down to go through a gated stile at Park End. Continue descending aiming for a gap in the centre of the wall opposite. Bear left and go through a gate, bear right and descend steeply towards the cottage on the right. At the cottage go through a gap in the wall to the left of the cottage and then descend through a gap stile onto the road.

10 *(GR: 000 985)* Turn right and continue along the road for about 300 yards (275m) to a left bend sign. Leave the road *(SP Isles Bridge)* and follow a narrow track down to the riverbank. Now follow a clear riverside path to Isles Bridge.

11 *(GR: 977 975)* Turn left and start to cross the bridge, after a few yards go through a gap stile on the right *(SP Footpath)* and descend some steps. Follow the river upstream, *(the right of way goes straight across the island)* cross a small stream and then a large meadow. Cross a wooden step stile and follow the right fence, passing an enclosure with a static caravan. Go through a gate *(SP Footpath)*, turn left and continue through a stile onto the main road.

12 *(GR: 969 975)* Turn left and follow the road for about 250 yards (230m). Leave the road along a narrow path which leads back to the riverside. Continue along the riverside over two stiles, climb up some steps and continue over a step stile returning briefly to the road.

13 *(GR: 960 979)* Turn left and immediately go through a gate on the left *(SP Footpath)*. Descend along a rough track and bear right, continue through ten gap stiles to Gunnerside. Turn right and follow the lane to the main road by the King's Head Inn. Turn left and return to the car park.

5

MAIDEN CASTLE and HARKERSIDE MOOR

from Reeth 8½ miles (14km)

This walk begins with an easy stroll along the banks of the river Swale. The scenery is rich in contrast and from Harkerside Moor there are some spectacular views of Swaledale and Arkengarthdale.

Reeth is an attractive village built around a large sloping green. It is situated at the foot of Calver Hill, with impressive views of the surrounding hills and wild moorland. The village has had its share of prosperity over the centuries and was important enough to be mentioned in the Domesday Book. In 1695 Reeth was granted a charter to hold a weekly market and four fairs each year. These continued to be held until the end of the nineteenth century, about the same time as the lead mines closed down. Nowadays, the village relies on tourism, but still holds its Annual Agricultural Show on the last Wednesday in August.

We leave Reeth along Quaker Lane, so called because of a Quaker school which existed nearby. It was endowed about 1785 by three brothers, George, Leonard and John Raw. The school was rebuilt on the hill above the village in 1862, with a legacy in the will of John Raw's son. The will stipulated that the school had to be visible from all the parishes which it served, hence its commanding position.

At the end of Quaker Lane we continue along a meadow path, rich in flowers, descending to the banks of the river Swale. The path follows the riverside and many species of birds may be seen. These include dipper, linnet, meadow pipit, red poll, sand martin and willow warbler. At the main road we continue to Scabba Wath Bridge.

This crossing of the Swale lies on the old Roman road which connected the forts at Bainbridge and Bowes.

After crossing the bridge we follow the road for a good mile before leaving it to climb up to Maiden Castle. Along the roadside there are large patches of juniper shrub. Juniper leaves are rich in aromatic oil and its berries are used both medicinally and as a flavouring. At one time there were hundreds of acres of juniper in Swaledale. During times of plague chips of juniper were burned to fumigate houses and few people would be without them.

Maiden Castle is an impressive hillside enclosure, forming a large irregular circle and measuring over 70 yards (66m) across. It is surrounded by a deep outer ditch and an internal bank, there are also traces of a rampart wall on the top bank. It has a single entrance to the east where large, roughly dressed stone blocks suggest a possible gatehouse. Leading away from the entrance is an avenue of stones some 110 feet (33m) in length. The original purpose of Maiden Castle is uncertain, although the rising land and dead ground to the south means that it was poorly sited for defensive purposes.

From the enclosure we climb up onto Harker Hill and continue across Harkerside Moor. Directly across the valley is Calver Hill with Healaugh nestling below and to the right lie Fremington Edge and Arkengarthdale. The magnificent views remain with us during the long descent to Grinton

The village of Grinton is situated on the south side of the river Swale near its confluence with Arkle Beck. The church, dedicated to St Andrew, was founded in the twelfth century by the Augustinian Canons of Bridlington Priory. It consists of nave, north and south aisles, south porch, chancel with side chapels and a low square tower containing six bells. There is a lepers' squint in the south chapel where lepers were able watch the church services. The pulpit is carved from oak with a sounding board dated 1718. Because of its great size it was known as 'The Cathedral of the Dales,' and is one of the largest parishes in the land.

We continue across Grinton Bridge and follow Arkle Beck to Reeth Bridge. Both these structures were the work of Bridge Master John Carr of York, whose major works include the Castle Museum at York and Harewood House near Leeds. Reeth Bridge was rebuilt in 1773 to replace one destroyed in the great flood two years earlier. The bridge at Grinton was widened by Carr in 1797. The road is now followed back to the village green.

Start/Parking:	Reeth, around the village green and also an overflow car park 100 yards (91m) along the Gunnerside road.
Location:	Reeth is situated 11 miles (17.5km) west of Richmond on the B6270 Richmond to Kirby Stephen road.
Grid Ref:	038 993.
Distance:	8½ miles (14km) circular. Allow 4½ hrs.
OS Maps:	Explorer OL30 (1:25,000) or Landranger 98 and 92 (1:50,000).
Refreshments:	The Black Bull, the Buck Hotel, the King's Arms, the Copper Kettle Restaurant and several tea shops.
Public Toilets:	Reeth, near the Buck Hotel.
Other:	Swaledale Folk Museum, shops, Post Office, bus service, telephone.

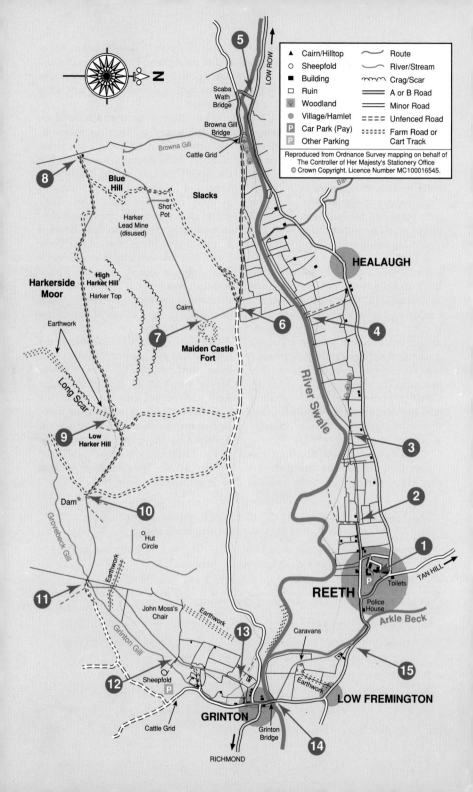

5 Maiden Castle and Harkerside Moor

1 *(GR: 038 993)* Leave Reeth at the corner of the green near the 'Pots 'n' Presents' gift shop and go past the 'Garden House Pottery' *(sign on wall - to the River)*. Turn left at the road junction and then turn right onto a narrow tarmac lane *(SP Swing Bridge)*. This is Quaker Lane. Follow the lane which becomes rougher after passing the doctor's surgery. Continue along the lane to a gate.

2 *(GR: 035 991)* Go through the stile on the right of the gate *(SP Healaugh)*. Follow the left wall and go through a gap stile. Go straight across the next field and continue through five more gap stiles.

3 *(GR: 028 991)* Head to the far left corner of the field and go through a gate. Cross the field to the banks of the river Swale, turn right and follow the river upstream.

4 *(GR: 021 988)* Cross two stiles and continue upstream crossing Barney Beck via some stepping stones. At the road, turn left and continue to Scabba Wath Bridge.

5 *(GR: 006 984)* Turn left *(Road sign - Askrigg 6½)* cross the bridge and turn left at the junction *(Road sign - Grinton 3)*. Follow the road, and after crossing a cattle grid begin climbing gradually for about 1 mile (1.3km).

6 *(GR: 020 983)* Leave the road *(SP Castle Bolton/Whitaside)*, DO NOT FOLLOW THE TRACK, instead follow a faint track to the left, climbing up through the heather towards a single hawthorn tree. Maiden Castle is to the left of the tree.

7 *(GR: 012 981)* From the fort climb up through the heather to the south-west, when a cairn comes into view, head directly for it. The path levels out and, although poorly defined, continues past the cairn eventually reaching a broad track. Cross the track and climb up towards a shooting hut on the horizon.

8 *(GR: 010 972)* Turn left and follow the track which climbs onto Harkerside Moor. Continue along the track to the earthworks at Long Scar.

9 *(GR: 028 974)* After passing through the earthworks descend gently to a junction of tracks.

10 *(GR: 032 972)* Leave the track and follow a clear path through the heather. Cross a beck and go through a gate in the fence.

11 *(GR: 039 972)* Follow the beck downstream for about 30 yards (28m) and then cross to the other side. Continue along a clear track climbing slightly to pass through the earthwork. Go through a gate and descend along a clear path towards Grinton.

12 *(GR: 044 979)* Go through the gate and follow the left wall through a gate to the left side of a barn. Head to the left slightly and descend through two fields.

13 *(GR: 045 983)* Turn right, go through two gates and descend to the road at Grinton. Turn left and follow the road past St Andrew's Church and over Grinton Bridge.

14 *(GR: 046 986)* Go through a gap stile and go through a gate near some static caravans. Turn right and follow a clear signposted path through two more gates to Fremington.

15 *(GR: 043 991)* Turn left and follow the road. Cross Reeth Bridge and return to the village centre.

SWALE HALL

Swale Hall, to the west of Grinton, was formerly the residence of a gentleman, who described himself as "Sir Solomon Swale, of Swale Hall, in Swaledale, fast by the river Swale". This family held Crown lands, but had omitted to renew their lease. This was discovered by a clerk in the exchequer office, he procured a grant from the Crown, giving him title to the estate. Several law suits ensued, but they only added to the misfortunes of Sir Solomon, who died in a debtors' prison, in 1733.

6

SURRENDER BRIDGE and CALVER HILL

from Langthwaite 8½ miles (14km)

Magnificent views, uplifting moorland and superb valley scenery are some of the rewards during this delightful walk. One of the highlights is the famous water-splash at Fore Gill Gate.

Langthwaite is regarded as the capital of Arkengarthdale. Its little stone cottages and its inn, the Red Lion, are crowded together round a small square. The name is of Norse origin and means 'the long clearing'. Before the Norman Conquest, Arkengarthdale was part of the estates of the Earls of Mercia. It was held by Arkil, the son of Gospatrick, whose name has been impressed on the beck and the dale.

After William the Conqueror's 'Harrying of the North', as it was later called, the Dales were left thinly populated. In the Domesday Book of 1086 most of the North Riding was written off as wasteland. However, Arkengarthdale, well covered by forest, was preserved by the Norman lords to fulfil their great passion for hunting. Special laws existed within the confines of the forest. The cutting of wood, clearing of land, grazing of livestock and keeping of dogs were very strictly controlled. Anyone who transgressed these laws was severely dealt with.

From the village we follow Arkle Beck to a wooden footbridge. After crossing the bridge a meadow path leads up to Arkle Town. Arkengarthdale's first church was built here in 1145, believed to have been given by Conan, Earl of Richmond, to Egglestone Abbey in Teesdale. Nothing remains of the church, demolished in 1818, except some dismal old tombstones, sloping at various angles.

After walking up through the village we join a path leading around Clumber Hill and above the steep gorge of Fore Gill. At Fore Gill Gate the road descends to the water-splash, which featured in the popular television series *All Creatures Great and Small*. James Herriot, the vet, was seen driving through it in one of the title sequences.

Our route continues along the road to the Surrender smelt mill. The mill, built about 1840, replaced two earlier mills on the site. It had three ore hearths and a slag hearth. These were arranged in pairs, set back-to-back and powered by a central water-wheel and bellows room. The water was brought along a leat from the beck, its course can be traced back to the road and for some distance upstream. Each pair of hearths had a common flue which joined with the main flue 40 to 50 feet (12 to 15m) above the mill. The main flue, 820 yards (750m) long, is visible on the hillside and continues beyond the road. It was roofed with flat slabs where it left the mill; higher up on the moor it was arched over. A roasting hearth was added later and the base of its chimney can be seen at the back wall of the furnace shop.

Leaving the smelt mill we continue over Bleaberry Gill and into the wooded valley above Barney Beck. The mixed woodland of birch, oak, sycamore and pine provides excellent shade for the woodland flowers, mainly bluebells, wood sorrel and yellow pimpernell.

From the wood a farm track leads up onto the open moor where we begin our crossing of the shapely Calver Hill, also known locally as Mount Calva. The name, generally accepted as meaning 'the hill where calves are pastured', may also have a religious origin. Some of the local people have carried on a tradition of having their ashes scattered on the summit. In 1937, one man had a limestone cross built close to the summit. It is named Gobat's Cross after him. Unfortunately the right of way passes below the summit, but the views are still outstanding.

During the descent to Arkle Beck there are excellent views of Fremington Edge and Booze Moor. After crossing the beck we follow it upstream through the meadows and return to Langthwaite.

Depending upon the season there are many wild flowers to watch out for including ragged robin, forget-me-not, brook lime, scurvy grass, marsh marigold, wood sage and rockrose. The bird life is also plentiful and the dipper will no doubt make an appearance. Chaffinch, grey wagtail, pied wagtail, goldfinch and wren may also be spotted.

Start/Parking:	Langthwaite, there is a small car park and also limited parking in the village square.
Location:	Langthwaite is situated 3 miles (5km) north-west of Reeth on the road to Tan Hill.
Grid Ref:	006 024.
Distance:	8½ miles (14km) circular. Allow 5 hrs.
OS Maps:	Explorer OL30 (1:25,000) or Landranger 92 (1:50,000).
Refreshments:	The Red Lion Inn and the Charles Bathurst Hotel at Langthwaite, Chapel Farm Tea Rooms at Whaw.
Public Toilets:	Langthwaite, opposite the Methodist chapel.
Other:	Methodist chapel, St Mary's Church, Post Office, telephone.

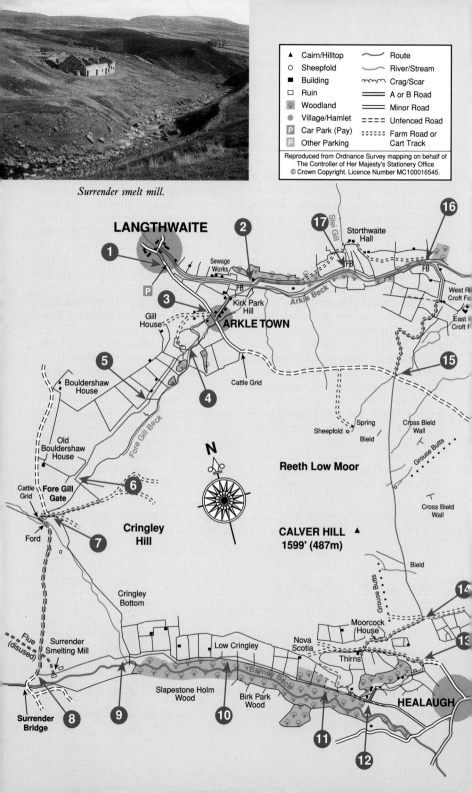

Surrender smelt mill.

Legend

▲	Cairn/Hilltop		Route
○	Sheepfold		River/Stream
■	Building		Crag/Scar
□	Ruin		A or B Road
🌲	Woodland		Minor Road
●	Village/Hamlet	====	Unfenced Road
🅿	Car Park (Pay)	····	Farm Road or Cart Track
🅿	Other Parking		

Reproduced from Ordnance Survey mapping on behalf of The Controller of Her Majesty's Stationery Office © Crown Copyright. Licence Number MC100016545.

LANGTHWAITE

Sewage Works

Storthwaite Hall

West R Croft Fa

East Croft F

FB

Slei Gill

Arkle Beck

ARKLE TOWN

Kirk Park Hill

Gill House

Bouldershaw House

Cattle Grid

Old Bouldershaw House

Fore Gill Beck

Cattle Grid

Fore Gill Gate

Ford

N

Cringley Hill

Reeth Low Moor

Sheepfold

Spring

Bield

Cross Bield Wall

Grouse Butts

Cross Bield Wall

CALVER HILL
1599' (487m)

Bield

Grouse Butts

Moorcock House

Nova Scotia

Thirns

HEALAUGH

Cringley Bottom

Flue (disused)

Surrender Smelting Mill

Low Cringley

Slapestone Holm Wood

Birk Park Wood

Barney Beck

Surrender Bridge

① ② ③ ④ ⑤ ⑥ ⑦ ⑧ ⑨ ⑩ ⑪ ⑫ ⑬ ⑭ ⑮ ⑯ ⑰

6   Surrender Bridge and Calver Hill

1 *(GR: 006 024)* Turn right out of the car park, then take the first road on the right *(sign Red Lion Inn)* and cross the bridge over Arkle Beck. At the Red Lion Inn, turn right onto the lane opposite, bear right to join a broad track and follow the beck downstream.

2 *(GR: 011 021)* Cross a footbridge over the beck, turn right and follow a clear path leading uphill and through a gap stile into the old graveyard. Continue through another stile in the wall opposite. Turn left and follow the road to the top of the village. Turn right along the road for about 40 yards (37m).

3 *(GR: 007 019)* Leave the road via a gap stile on the left *(SP Fore Gill Gate 1½)*. Cross the field and go through a gap stile to the right of a barn. Follow the left wall round and go through a gap in the wall. Continue beside the wall passing around Clumber Hill to a signpost *(SP Public Footpath)*.

4 *(GR: 005 018)* Go through two gap stiles, climbing slightly to the right to pass over the hill. Cross a small stream and pass through a broken wall. Continue beside the right fence/wall across three fields.

5 *(GR: 002 015)* Staying close to the right wall, continue through the bracken. At the wall corner continue straight ahead on a clear path across the open moorland climbing slightly and returning to the wall side.

6 *(GR: 995 012)* Turn left and descend to a gap stile in the wall opposite, by the fence. Climb up through the heather to a broad track. Turn right and follow the track to Fore Gill Gate.

7 *(GR: 993 010)* Go through the gate, turn left and follow the road downhill. Cross a cattle grid and the water-splash *(a footbridge is provided)*. Follow the road to Surrender Bridge.

8 *(GR: 990 000)* Turn left and leave the road *(SP Footpath)*. Continue along a clear track passing between the smelt mill and the peat store. Climb onto the ridge and follow a good path.

9 *(GR: 996 999)* Descend a steep path and cross the beck. Continue through a gap stile and follow the right wall through the wood.

10 *(GR: 003 997)* Leave the wood via a gap in the wall, turn right *(SP Footpath)* and continue through the fields passing below Nova Scotia to re-enter the woodland. Remain close to the right wall through the wood.

11 *(GR: 009 993)* On leaving the wood continue beside the wall and pass through two gap stiles. Turn right and follow a forest track.

12 *(GR: 011 992)* Turn left and follow the driveway, go over a stile in the fence immediately after the first building on the right. Continue with the left wall and go through a gate. Bear half right and follow the wall round to a gap stile. Cross the field and go through a gate to the right of the farm. Turn right and go through another gate. Follow an enclosed track climbing to the left and go through a gate onto the road.

13 *(GR: 016 993)* Turn left and follow the road uphill. At a junction turn right and continue climbing along a concrete track passing Moorcock House.

14 *(GR: 016 996)* Leave the track *(SP Footpath)* turning left to follow a path over the shoulder of Calver Hill. After passing a line of grouse butts bear slightly right and continue down to the main road.

15 *(GR: 018 012)* Cross the road and follow the farm track downhill through a gate to West Raw Croft Farm. Go through a gate to the left of the farm and follow an enclosed green lane down and through another gate to Arkle Beck.

16 *(GR: 022 019)* Cross the footbridge, turn left and follow the beck upstream via a wooden stile, a gate and a footbridge at Slei Gill.

17 *(GR: 017 020)* From the footbridge continue upstream, go through a tunnel and follow a broad track which leads back to Langthwaite.

7

WHAW and
DALE HEAD MOOR

from Langthwaite 8 miles (13km)

This is a splendid walk visiting some of Arkengarthdale's most secluded outposts. It has a good combination of meadow and moorland tracks, with some excellent scenery.

Arkengarthdale was once part of a vast feudal estate, later known as the Honour of Richmond. In 1071 this was granted to Alan Rufus, Count of Brittany. It was given as a reward for his services at the Battle of Hastings and for his help in suppressing the North's rebellion to Norman rule. The estate had 440 manors throughout England, one of the largest to be granted by William. It remained in the possession of the successive earls until 1435, when it reverted to the Crown.

The manor remained in the possession of the Crown until 1629, when Charles I granted it to Edward Ditchfield and others

in trust for the Citizens of London. It was acquired by Dr John Bathurst in 1656. He developed a thriving lead mining industry naming it the CB Company after his son, Charles. As the industry expanded, so did the population. At one time there were five inns, four alehouses, one church and six chapels serving the needs of the community. Most people worked for the CB Company. The mines closed in the late nineteenth century, mainly due to cheap imports of lead from abroad.

The walk begins with an easy stroll through the village past the Methodist chapel, St Mary's Church and the CB Hotel. The hexagonal building in the field near the junction to Barnard Castle was the powder house for the CB Company. It is one of the few remaining structures from the mining era and has survived intact. Farther along the road is the former CB yard. This group of buildings, arranged in a triangular shape, was built to house workers for the lead industry. It also contained a sawmill, stores, stables and homes for other estate employees.

From the road we descend along a clear track to cross Arkle Beck which we follow upstream to the peaceful hamlet of Whaw. That peace was interrupted in 1986 when 'Hurricane Charley' passed. Heavy rain on the moors turned Arkle Beck into a powerful and destructive force, causing it to rise 12 feet (3.5m) above normal. The top of Whaw's bridge was washed away and cottages at Langthwaite were flooded to a depth of 2 feet (0.6m).

Continuing upstream we pass through Low Faggergill and begin a gradual climb to Dale Head Farm, where a farm road leads round to Ravens Park Farm and onto open moorland.

There are many moorland birds to watch out for. The snipe will usually be seen probing into the wet ground for worms with its long straight bill. The song of the snipe has earned it the country name of 'heather bleater', which has nothing to do with its voice. As the male plunges through the air with tail outspread, the two outer tail feathers vibrate to produce the sound. It is usually heard, as part of the bird's courtship behaviour, between late March and the middle of June. Britain's largest wader, the curlew, as well as lapwings, redshanks and skylarks are also very likely to be spotted.

We continue across Gale Head Moor, climbing to High Faggergill and descend via Kitley Hill to the Whaw-Eskeleth road. As we walk along the road to High Eskeleth the views of the surrounding hills are excellent and there is also a bird's eye view of the CB yard, passed earlier in the walk.

Eskeleth is a tiny hamlet situated away from the main road. Its name means 'the hillside covered in ash trees'. Until the 1890s, one of the major drove roads from the Scottish Highlands passed through Eskeleth. Each year thousands of cattle were driven south to feed the growing populations of the industrial towns of England. This method of transporting cattle survived until the introduction of refrigeration, after which time animals were slaughtered locally. The meat was distributed where it was most needed, and more economically.

From Eskeleth we continue over Arkle Beck to the road near Stang Bridge. After crossing the road, we follow a quiet tarmac lane through the meadows to Langthwaite and return to the car park.

Start/Parking:	Langthwaite, there is a small car park and also limited parking in the village square.
Location:	Langthwaite is situated 3 miles (5km) north-west of Reeth on the road to Tan Hill.
Grid Ref:	006 024.
Distance:	8 miles (13km) circular. Allow 4 hrs.
OS Maps:	Explorer OL30 (1:25,000) or Landranger 92 (1:50,000).
Refreshments:	The Red Lion Inn and the Charles Bathurst Hotel at Langthwaite, Chapel Farm Tea Rooms at Whaw.
Public Toilets:	Langthwaite, opposite the Methodist chapel.
Other:	Methodist chapel, St Mary's Church, Post Office, telephone.

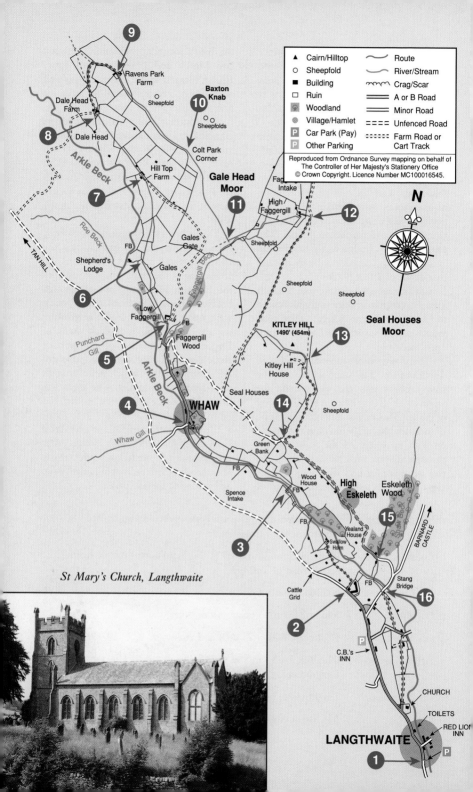

Legend

▲	Cairn/Hilltop	～ Route
○	Sheepfold	～ River/Stream
■	Building	⌒⌒⌒ Crag/Scar
□	Ruin	═══ A or B Road
🌳	Woodland	═══ Minor Road
●	Village/Hamlet	==== Unfenced Road
P	Car Park (Pay)	···· Farm Road or Cart Track
P	Other Parking	

Reproduced from Ordnance Survey mapping on behalf of The Controller of Her Majesty's Stationery Office © Crown Copyright. Licence Number MC100016545.

N

Ravens Park Farm
Baxton Knab
Dale Head Farm
Sheepfold
Dale Head
Sheepfolds
Arkle Beck
Colt Park Corner
Hill Top Farm
Gale Head Moor
Roe Beck
Gales Gate
Fag... Intake
High Faggergill
TAN HILL
FB
Shepherd's Lodge
Gales
Sheepfold
Faggergill Beck
Seal Houses Moor
Low Faggergill
FB
Sheepfold
Sheepfold
Punchard Gill
Faggergill Wood
KITLEY HILL 1490' (454m)
Arkle Beck
Kitley Hill House
WHAW
Seal Houses
Sheepfold
Whaw Gill
Green Bank
FB
Eskeleth Wood
Wood House
High Eskeleth
Spence Intake
FB
Yealand House
Stang Beck
BARNARD CASTLE
Swallow Holm
Stang Bridge
Cattle Grid
C.B.'s INN
CHURCH
TOILETS
RED LION INN
LANGTHWAITE

St Mary's Church, Langthwaite

7 Whaw and Dale Head Moor

1 *(GR: 006 024)* From the car park turn right and follow the road out of the village passing St Mary's Church and the Charles Bathurst Hotel. Continue straight on at the road junction *(towards Tan Hill)* and pass the former CB yard.

2 *(GR: 997 035)* Leave the road through a gap stile *(SP footpath)* and follow a stone track down to a cottage. Go through two gates to the left of the cottage, head towards the right boundary and descend to the beck side. Follow the beck upstream and cross a footbridge, climb up to the left and follow a clear path through a derelict wall. Proceed over a wooden walkway via two step stiles and follow the fence to a footbridge.

3 *(GR: 991 041)* Cross the wooden stile and the footbridge over Arkle Beck. Go through a gap stile on the left and follow the beck upstream through the wood. Continue upstream through the meadows to Whaw.

4 *(GR: 983 045)* Follow the road through the village passing the Chapel Farm Tea Rooms *(last chance for refreshments)*. At a right bend leave the road and go through a gate on the left *(sign Low Faggergill)*. Proceed along a good tarmac lane uphill.

5 *(GR: 980 052)* When the tarmac lane ends take the left fork and go through a gate on the left before the farm buildings. Bear right and go through a gate, climb up to a gap stile in the wall opposite. Proceed across the field and cross a walled lane, head towards the far right corner of the field and go through a gap stile.

6 *(GR: 978 056)* Bear left, pass a wall end and head for a gate in the centre of the wall. Go through the gate and bear right towards Hill Top Farm.

7 *(GR: 976 062)* Join the farm track coming from right and follow it through a gate, pass between the barn and the farmhouse and go through another gate. Follow the right wall, pass through a gate and head diagonally across two fields to Dale Head Farm.

8 *(GR: 972 066)* Go through two gates passing in front of the farmhouse. Turn right, go through a gate and follow a concrete road climbing up through two further gates to Ravens Park.

9 *(GR: 973 069)* Pass in front of the farmhouse and go through a gate at the end of a walled track. Continue close to the right wall passing through two more gates.

10 *(GR: 979 064)* *(This section of the walk is the most difficult to follow)*. From the wall corner bear right slightly to cross the open moor. When the path fades out continue on roughly the same heading and descend to a stream.

11 *(GR: 983 059)* Turn left and proceed upstream. Go through a gap stile by a gate and bear left to a ladder stile near the centre of the left wall. From the ladder stile head to the far right corner of the field. Go through two gates to the right of the farmhouse, turn right and follow the farm road to join a good stone track.

12 *(GR: 989 061)* Turn right and continue along the stone track. Just before reaching a wall on the left, turn left and begin climbing towards Kitley Hill, keeping close to the wall. Pass below the summit of Kitley Hill.

13 *(GR: 991 051)* Go through a gate, turn right and join a rough farm track which descends to the Whaw/Eskeleth road.

14 *(GR: 990 045)* Turn left and follow the road through Eskeleth.

15 *(GR: 999 038)* Go through a gap stile on the right *(SP footpath)* and descend to cross a footbridge over Arkle Beck. Turn left and follow the beck downstream, go through a gap stile and cross the road.

16 *(GR: 000 035)* Continue along a tarmac road which leads through three meadows to St Mary's Church. Turn left at the road and return to the car park by the outward route.

MARRICK PRIORY and the NUNS' CAUSEY

from Downholme Bridge 7½ miles (12km)

Wild flowers and birds are well represented during this lovely walk. It follows well defined paths through meadows and woodland, and the scenery is excellent.

Until the building of Downholme Bridge, towards the end of the seventeenth century, no roads crossed the river Swale between Grinton and Richmond. All traffic had to use the steeper road passing through Marske. In 1684, John Hutton of Marske, asked permission to make a bridge across the Swale 'betwixt Dounham and Maske', offering to pay a great part of the cost. This bridge was destroyed during the great flood of 1771 and rebuilt two years later by bridge master John Carr of York. It has three semicircular arches with a overall span of 56 yards (51m) and the width is 13 feet (4m).

After crossing the bridge we follow the road for a short distance and then continue through the fields to Hollins Farm. At the farm we join the Coast-to-Coast footpath which leads through lush meadows to Marrick. Standing at just over 1000 feet (305m) Marrick is endowed with some splendid views of Lower Swaledale and its beautiful woodland.

From Marrick a flagged path, known as the Nuns' Causey, descends through Steps Wood to Marrick Priory. The causey is supposed to have 375 steps. However, many of them are irregular and hard to distinguish. Steps Wood is a haven for birds, both the great spotted and green woodpeckers are well established. The nuthatch, willow warbler, wood warbler and spotted flycatcher also nest here. The nuthatch gets its name from its habit of wedging nuts in the bark of a tree and splitting them open with vigorous blows from its 'hatchet' bill. It is also the only British bird that regularly climbs down trees headfirst.

Marrick Priory was founded by Roger de Aske in 1154 as a house for Benedictine nuns. It was the richest nunnery in Yorkshire, but still poor when compared to the male religious houses. Marrick was dissolved in 1540, at which time it had a prioress and sixteen nuns. All that remains of the original structure is the tower. The nave was rebuilt in 1811 and services are still held there from time to time. The priory is now used as a training centre for the Diocese of Ripon and Leeds.

Our walk continues to join an enclosed lane, where the remains of Ellerton Priory can be seen across the river. Ellerton was a Cistercian nunnery, one of the smallest and, unlike Marrick, one of the poorest in England. Its origin is uncertain, having been ransacked by Scottish raiders who destroyed all its records. The nuns, who lived in perpetual silence, never exceeded thirteen in number and were drawn from the most respectable families. Ellerton succumbed to the first Act of Dissolution, closing in 1536, when there were five nuns including the prioress, who surrendered it 'without murmure or griefe'. Both priories were actively involved in the wool trade and had business dealings with Florentine merchants. They referred to Marrick as 'Marriche in Chosta Ricciamont' and Ellerton as 'Ellertana'.

The priory is sited within the grounds of Ellerton Abbey, a regency villa, built c.1830 for the Erle-Drax family. The house has had many uses; a family home, shooting lodge, army hospital and it was featured in the popular television series 'All Creatures Great and Small' as the home of Mrs Pumphrey and Tricki-Woo!

The lane leads back to Marrick where we begin our return to Downholme Bridge. During early summer there is a constant carpet of colour in the hay meadows beside the path; buttercups, knapweed, pignut and yellow rattle are most common.

After crossing Oxque Beck a riverside path leads to the road. This is another excellent spot for birds and dipper, goldfinch, grey wagtail and swallow all take advantage of this pleasant stretch of the river Swale. Small flocks of goldfinches, aptly known as 'charms', may be spotted feeding on the heads of thistles and other tall weeds during late summer and autumn. In Victorian times goldfinches were sought after as songbirds. Records from 1860 show that more than 132,000 birds a year were being taken by the cage-bird trade.

Start/Parking:	Downholme Bridge, there is a large layby on the A6108 close to the bridge.
Location:	Downholme Bridge is situated 4½ miles (7.2km) west of Richmond just off the A6108 road.
Grid Ref:	113 992.
Distance:	7½ miles (12km) circular. Allow 4 hrs.
OS Maps:	Explorer OL30 (1:25,000) or Landranger 99 (1:50,000).
Refreshments:	None on route.
Public Toilets:	None on route. The nearest are at the Round Howe car park off the A6108 near Richmond.
Other:	Post Office and telephone at Marske.

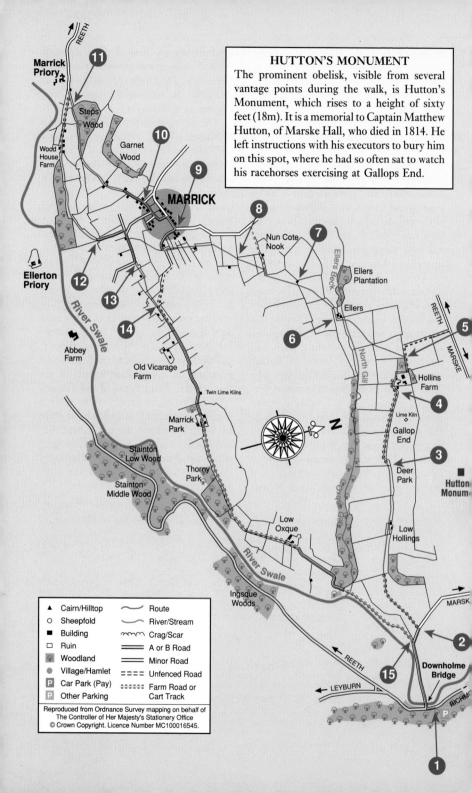

REETH

Marrick Priory ▲

11

Steps Wood

Wood House Farm

Garnet Wood

10

Ellerton Priory

MARRICK

9

8

Nun Cote Nook

7

Ellers Beck

Ellers Plantation

6

Ellers

12

13

14

River Swale

Abbey Farm

Old Vicarage Farm

Twin Lime Kilns

Marrick Park

Stainton Low Wood

Thorny Park

Stainton Middle Wood

Low Oxque

River Swale

Ingsque Woods

North Gill

Oxque Gill

REETH

MARSKE

5

Hollins Farm

4

Lime Kiln

Gallop End

3

Deer Park

Low Hollings

Hutton Monum...

N

2

MARSK...

LEYBURN

REETH

15

Downholme Bridge

RICHMO...

P

1

HUTTON'S MONUMENT

The prominent obelisk, visible from several vantage points during the walk, is Hutton's Monument, which rises to a height of sixty feet (18m). It is a memorial to Captain Matthew Hutton, of Marske Hall, who died in 1814. He left instructions with his executors to bury him on this spot, where he had so often sat to watch his racehorses exercising at Gallops End.

Symbol	Description	Symbol	Description
▲	Cairn/Hilltop	～	Route
○	Sheepfold	～	River/Stream
■	Building	︿︿︿	Crag/Scar
□	Ruin	═══	A or B Road
🌲	Woodland	═══	Minor Road
●	Village/Hamlet	====	Unfenced Road
P	Car Park (Pay)	······	Farm Road or Cart Track
P	Other Parking		

Reproduced from Ordnance Survey mapping on behalf of The Controller of Her Majesty's Stationery Office © Crown Copyright. Licence Number MC100016545.

8 Marrick Priory and the Nuns' Steps

1 *(GR: 113 992)* From the parking place walk south along the A6108 main road to the road junction *(SP Marrick Priory, Marske)*. Turn right and cross Downholme Bridge. Continue along the road ascending gently and go round a bend in the road to a bridleway on the left *(ignore the first bridleway this is the return route)*.

2 *(GR: 108 993)* Go through the gate *(SP Bridleway)*, follow a clear track, climbing towards the wood on the right. Go through a gate and follow the right wall through three large fields.

3 *(GR: 098 994)* The track becomes stonier and more distinct. Staying close to the wall continue through three more fields to Hollins Farm.

4 *(GR: 093 995)* Follow the track round to the left of the farmhouse, passing through a gate and continue to another gate. STOP! DO NOT USE IT, instead turn left and follow the boundary to a gap in the wall. Go through the gap and follow the right boundary across the wooded area and go through a gate. Turn left and continue along a good farm track beside the wood.

5 *(GR: 091 996)* Go through a gate on the left, follow a clear track, descending diagonally across the field and pass through a gate in the bottom right corner. Continue descending towards Ellers, cross the beck by a wooden footbridge, go through a gap stile and follow the wall to its corner

6 *(GR: 087 992)* Turn right *(SP Footpath)* pass in front of Ellers Cottage and go through a gap stile *(SP Footpath)*. Continue across the meadow and go through another gap stile. Head diagonally towards a barn in the left corner of the field.

7 *(GR: 084 990)* Go through a gate to the left of the barn *(SP Footpath)*, climb steeply towards the top right corner of the field. Turn right at the wall corner *(SP Bridleway/Footpath)*. Go through a gate onto a farm road, immediately go through a gate on the left *(SP Footpath)*. Climb steeply to cross a stile in a fence and go through a gap stile in the top right corner of the field.

8 *(GR: 081 987)* The path levels out, cross two meadows diagonally, now follow the right boundary and go through a gap stile. Continue via four more gap stiles onto a stone track which leads to the road, turn right and follow the road to a junction.

9 *(GR: 079 983)* Turn left and follow the road to a telephone box, turn left and continue round to a T-Junction.

10 *(GR: 076 981)* Go straight on *(SP Marrick Priory, Reeth)*. At the Wesleyan chapel pass through a gate and follow the left wall through three more gates into Steps Wood. Descend a flagged causeway through the wood and leave it via a gate.

11 *(GR: 069 977)* Continue down through a gate onto the road. Turn left and follow the road past some caravans and climb slightly to Wood House Farm. After passing the farmhouse the track becomes rougher and steeper as it climbs back to Marrick.

12 *(GR: 078 978)* Go through a gate onto an enclosed green track *(SP Bridleway)* and continue climbing towards Marrick. At the top turn right onto a tarmac road. After about 20 yards (18m), at a bend, leave the road to follow a clear stone track.

13 *(GR: 080 980)* When the track turns sharp right leave it and go through a gap stile ahead. Follow a clear path through four more gap stiles and join a stone track coming down from the left.

14 *(GR: 083 981)* Navigation should now be easy as this track leads all the way back to the road near Downholme Bridge.

15 *(GR: 109 992)* Go through the gate, turn right and follow the outward route back to the car.

ORGATE FORCE and SKELTON MOOR

from Marske 7½ miles (12km)

This walk explores the beautiful side valley of Marske Beck. The mixture of moorland and woodland scenery is excellent and the gradients are gentle.

Marske is a secluded village, set in luxuriant woodland surroundings, sitting astride the 'old road' from Reeth to Richmond. The imposing Marske Hall, now divided into private flats, was built about 1735 for the distinguished Hutton family. They provided two Archbishops of York, the second one progressing to become Archbishop of Canterbury in 1757.

The church, dedicated to St Edmund the Martyr, dates from 1090 and traces of the original structure are still visible, including the Norman door arches. It comprises a nave, north aisle, south porch and chancel. At the west end is a small bell cote, with two ancient bells. The church was restored in 1830, at the expense of John Hutton Esq, when the chancel was rebuilt and most of the interior fittings of the church renewed. A marble tablet, surmounted by a bust, has been placed in the chancel to his memory.

The route out of the village follows a broad track passing through the sylvan paradise of Clints Wood. The wood, mainly ash and sycamore, is enriched with wild flowers, especially in summer, when foxgloves, rose bay willow herb and bluebells provide a feast of colour. It is also teeming with wild birds, chaffinch, dunnock and wren are the most likely to be seen, as well as summer visitors such as blackcap and chiffchaff. The blackcap's rich and melodious song has won it the reputation as the 'northern nightingale'. Its cap, black in the male and red-brown in the female, makes it easy to identify.

After leaving the wood a broad green path leads to Orgate Farm, where we descend to cross Marske Beck. Orgate Force can be seen further upstream, but a short detour along the bank will yield a much better view of this striking waterfall. Our walk continues along the valley floor to Telfit Farm.

Near the end of the last Ice Age the Stainmore glacier advanced into Swaledale at Telfit, grinding out the deep channels of Marske Beck. When the glacier began to melt, the debris it had been carrying was left behind to create a terminal moraine or dam across the valley. Behind this the melt waters were trapped and a glacial lake formed. The river eventually cut its way through the softer boulder clay and drained the lake.

Shortly after passing Telfit we rejoin Marske Beck and continue upstream to the tiny hamlet of Helwith. This was a much larger settlement during the lead mining era. But nowadays only a few cottages and the former manor house remain. From Helwith we follow the banks of Shaw Beck, passing some of the old mine workings which include a row of eleven ore bunkers. Ore was stored here prior to crushing and washing. Each bunker held the ore of one partnership of six to eight miners known as bouse teams. Grey and pied wagtails, meadow pipits and wheatears are often spotted along this quiet stretch. The grey wagtail, in spite of its name, is one of the most colourful of the wagtails. Its bright yellow underparts contrast boldly with its blue-grey back and long black tail.

Just above the mine workings we cross a small packhorse bridge and begin an easy ascent out of the valley, leading onto the heather-clad Skelton Moor. The track across the moor was formerly an old lead road, used to transport ore from the Hurst lead mines for processing in the smelt mills at Clints.

The views from the top of Telfit Bank are exquisite, with Marske Beck winding its way through the meadows and woods in the valley below. Hutton's Monument provides a good landmark ahead. At Skelton the road leads downhill to Marske, but a more pleasant return is the field path crossing Pillimire Bridge. This packhorse bridge is situated away from the main road and has survived intact.

Above the bridge is a well preserved water-wheel, built to generate electricity for Skelton Hall. However, it is unlikely that a water-wheel, unlike a turbine, could have provided sufficient power for this purpose.

Start/Parking:	Marske, near the junction by the bridge or farther up the road heading towards Reeth.
Location:	Marske is situated 6 miles (9.6km) west of Richmond off the A6108 road.
Grid Ref:	104 004.
Distance:	7½ miles (12km) circular. Allow 4 hrs.
OS Maps:	Explorer OL30 (1:25,000) or Landranger 92 (1:50,000).
Refreshments:	None on route.
Public Toilets:	None on route. The nearest are at the Round Howe car park off the A6108 near Richmond.
Other:	Post Office, telephone.

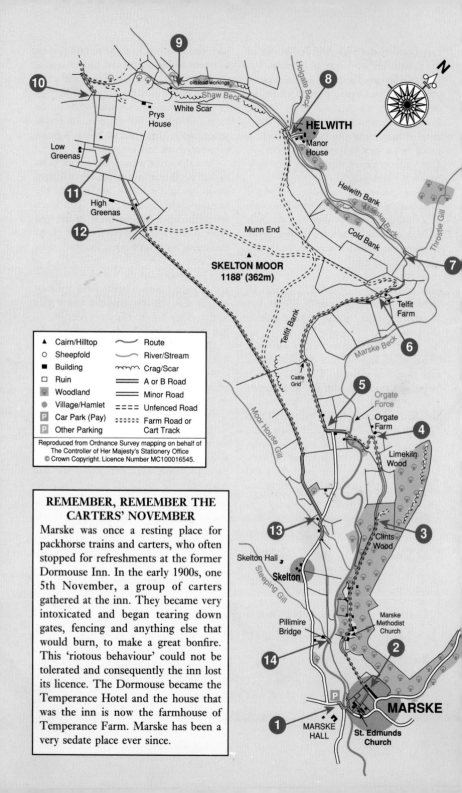

N

old lead workings

9

10

Shaw Beck

White Scar

Prys House

Holgate Beck

8

HELWITH

Manor House

Low Greenas

Helwith Bank

11

High Greenas

Munn End

Marskel Beck

Cold Bank

12

SKELTON MOOR
1188' (362m)

Telfit Bank

Throstle Gill

7

Telfit Farm

6

Marske Beck

Cattle Grid

5

Orgate Force

Orgate Farm

4

Limekiln Wood

Moor House Gill

3

Clints Wood

13

Skelton Hall

SKELTON

Steeping Gill

Marske Methodist Church

Pillimire Bridge

2

14

1

P

MARSKE HALL

MARSKE

St. Edmunds Church

▲	Cairn/Hilltop	～	Route
○	Sheepfold	～	River/Stream
■	Building	⌒⌒⌒	Crag/Scar
□	Ruin	═══	A or B Road
🌲	Woodland	══	Minor Road
●	Village/Hamlet	====	Unfenced Road
P	Car Park (Pay)	······	Farm Road or
P	Other Parking		Cart Track

Reproduced from Ordnance Survey mapping on behalf of
The Controller of Her Majesty's Stationery Office
© Crown Copyright. Licence Number MC100016545.

REMEMBER, REMEMBER THE CARTERS' NOVEMBER

Marske was once a resting place for packhorse trains and carters, who often stopped for refreshments at the former Dormouse Inn. In the early 1900s, one 5th November, a group of carters gathered at the inn. They became very intoxicated and began tearing down gates, fencing and anything else that would burn, to make a great bonfire. This 'riotous behaviour' could not be tolerated and consequently the inn lost its licence. The Dormouse became the Temperance Hotel and the house that was the inn is now the farmhouse of Temperance Farm. Marske has been a very sedate place ever since.

9 Orgate Force and Skelton Moor

1 *(GR: 104 004)* Follow the road over the bridge and climb uphill towards the village centre. Leave the road via some steps leading into St Edmund's churchyard. Pass to the left of the church and go through a gate, continue across a driveway and then go through two gap stiles leading onto a side road.

2 *(GR: 104 006)* Turn left and follow the road through a gate onto a stone track and over a cattle grid. Proceed along a the track which leads through Clints Wood.

3 *(GR: 096 015)* At a fork, towards the end of the wood, take the narrower track on the left *(Bridleway marker)*. Leave the wood via a gate and follow an enclosed green lane to Orgate Farm.

4 *(GR: 092 018)* Turn left and follow the concrete road downhill to cross Orgate Bridge *(Orgate Force can be seen through the trees further upstream)*. Continue along the road climbing to a barn, go straight ahead with the right wall. After a few yards the road becomes a rough farm road. Follow the road round to a gate.

5 *(GR: 090 016)* Go through the gate *(sign Telfit Farm Private Road)* and continue along the track crossing one cattle grid to reach Telfit Farm.

6 *(GR: 086 025)* At the farm, take the left fork climbing through a gate. When the track doubles back, leave it and follow the right wall to go through a gate/gap. Continue ahead and over a slight ridge, then descend to Marske Beck.

7 *(GR: 086 028)* Go through the gate *(Footpath Marker)* and follow a clear green path upstream to Helwith.

8 *(GR: 074 029)* Ignore the footbridge, go through a gap in the wall and follow the fence. Go through a gate and ford the beck *(Shaw Beck)*, proceed upstream through a gap stile. After passing some old lead workings, cross the beck via a stone arched bridge.

9 *(GR: 066 025)* Continue upstream, pass in front of the ruin and cross to the right bank of the stream. Climb to the top of the valley and go through a gate. Follow the track round to the left and go through a gate. Proceed along the right boundary *(a little sketchy)* onto a stone farm track. Turn right and follow the track.

10 *(GR: 063 021)* When the left wall almost merges with the track, double back and follow the wall to its corner *(about 50 yards (46m))*. Turn right and go through a gate *(Bridleway markers)*. Head towards the left wall, climbing up to the right of a barn and go through a gate in the top fence. Turn left and follow the fence to its corner.

11 *(GR: 066 019)* Turn right and proceed towards the wall at the far side of the field. Go through a gate and follow the right wall through two gates passing between the barns. Continue along an enclosed track passing to the right of a large pond.

12 *(GR: 071 017)* Go through two gates *(crossing a tarmac lane end - the Helwith Road)*. Continue ahead on a clear path through the heather close to the right wall. After passing through a gate the track becomes broader, continue through another gate where the track becomes enclosed and leads down to the road.

13 *(GR: 094 012)* Turn right and follow the road down to a barn on the left. Go through the stile beside it and head diagonally across the field to cross a wooden stile in a fence. Follow the left fence over another stile and descend to Pillimire Bridge.

14 *(GR: 100 007)* Cross a wooden stile and turn left, cross the bridge. *(There is a gate at the exit to the bridge)*. Bear right and leave the beckside for a time and follow a faint path over a slight hill. Descend to a gate and go down a few steps, turn left and after about 30 yards (27m) climb some steps leading to a stile at Marske Bridge. Turn right, cross the bridge and return to the car.

WILLANCE'S LEAP and ROUND HOWE

from Richmond 7½ miles (12km)

Most of this beautiful walk lies outside the National Park boundary. However, it offers an excellent variety of scenery and is fairly easy after the initial climb to Whitcliffe Scar.

Richmond, rightfully regarded as the capital of Swaledale, is one of Yorkshire's most romantic and historic towns. The castle, which dominates the town, was built shortly after the Norman Conquest to establish the permanency of Norman rule in the North. It stands on a natural stronghold of rock, the defences forming a triangle, one side made impregnable by steep cliffs overhanging the river Swale and the other two defended by strong, lofty walls. The enormous keep was erected in 1146 and its walls reach a height of almost 100 feet (30m).

According to legend, King Arthur, with all his knights, rests in a secret chamber beneath the castle; sleeping, but ready to rise up should England need them again. The tradition was, the king and his knights would be aroused if a champion could find his way into the chamber, blow a horn that was lying near the king, and cut a garter with the sword lying beside him. A story is told of a man called Potter Thompson, who was exploring a cave under the castle and found the slumbering knights. He began to draw the sword from its scabbard, but, when the company began to stir he put it hastily back and fled for his life. No one has been able to find the cave since.

From Richmond we follow a long, quiet road climbing steadily to Whitcliffe Farm. After passing the farm we ascend through the fields to Whitcliffe Scar. The views are magnificent with the narrow gorge of the river Swale winding its way between steep wooded slopes. Looking back, there is a sensational view of Richmond, with the Vale of Mowbray, Hambleton Hills and the North York Moors beyond.

We continue along the top of the scar to Willance's Leap, where an amazing event took place in 1606. Robert Willance, a Richmond draper, was out hunting one day when a thick fog suddenly came down. His horse, an inexperienced and nervous young mare, bolted and leaped over the edge of Whitcliffe Scar, falling 200 feet (60m). The horse was killed instantly, but luck was on Willance's side, he suffered only a broken leg, which unfortunately was later amputated. Realising he would not be rescued until the fog lifted, he cut open the horse's belly and inserted his injured leg. This action most likely saved his life, as the extra warmth would have delayed the onset of gangrene. Three stones mark the last three strides the horse made, each bearing the inscription: '1606. Glory be to our merciful God who miraculously preserved me from the danger so great'.

From Willance's Leap we follow a clear path to the head of Deepdale where we begin our descent to the banks of the river Swale. Deepdale is a fine example of a dry valley. At the end of the last Ice Age, the ground remained partly frozen to great depths, preventing water from sinking down. Vast quantities of water from the melting ice surged down over the frozen rock cutting wedge shaped gorges into the valley sides. When the ground thawed out the water sank down through the rocks leaving the gorges dry.

Our route continues along the riverside to Whitcliffe Woods. Many wild birds nest here including the great spotted and the green woodpecker. The woods are also a haven for a variety of wild flowers, shrubs and trees. From Lownethwaite Farm a quiet lane leads to the main road where we continue to the car park at Round Howe, and cross a large footbridge.

Round Howe is a conical hill rising out of an immense basin of rock, the sides of which are covered with trees. The river Swale originally flowed on the opposite side of the howe, but the continual erosion by the river gradually cut through the neck of land on the north side, creating the present channel. After this the old channel slowly silted up to form this remarkable natural phenomenon.

After a pleasant walk along the riverside we arrive at Richmond Bridge and proceed via the market place back to the car park. If time allows a visit to Richmond Castle is a must, especially on a fine day.

Start/Parking:	Richmond, has several car parks, but for this walk use the Nuns' Close car park off Hurgill Road, just off the A6108.
Location:	Richmond is situated on the A6108 road 4½ miles (7.2km) south-west of Scotch Corner.
Grid Ref:	171 009.
Distance:	7½ miles (12km) circular. Allow 4 hrs.
OS Maps:	Explorer 304 (1:25,000) or Landranger 92 (1:50,000).
Refreshments:	Inns, cafes and restaurants in Richmond.
Public Toilets:	The car park, the market place and others in Richmond, also at Round Howe car park.
Other:	Shops, bus services, Post Office, the Green Howards Museum, the Georgian Theatre, the Friary Gardens, Richmond Castle and Saturday is 'market day'.

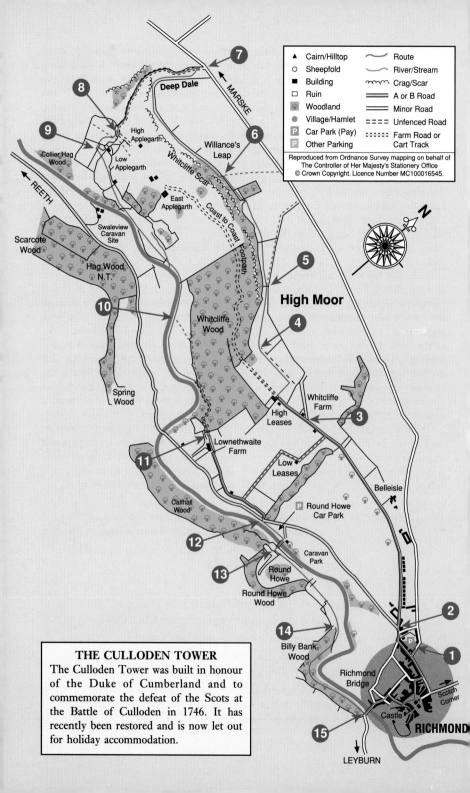

Legend

- ▲ Cairn/Hilltop
- ○ Sheepfold
- ■ Building
- □ Ruin
- 🏚 Woodland
- ● Village/Hamlet
- 🅿 Car Park (Pay)
- 🅿 Other Parking
- ～ Route
- ～ River/Stream
- ⌒⌒⌒ Crag/Scar
- ═══ A or B Road
- ── Minor Road
- ==== Unfenced Road
- ···· Farm Road or Cart Track

Reproduced from Ordnance Survey mapping on behalf of The Controller of Her Majesty's Stationery Office © Crown Copyright. Licence Number MC100016545.

MARSKE

Deep Dale

Willance's Leap

Whitcliffe Scar

High Applegarth

Low Applegarth

Collier Hag Wood

East Applegarth

REETH

Swaleview Caravan Site

Scarcote Wood

Hag Wood N.T.

Whitcliffe Wood

High Moor

Spring Wood

Whitcliffe Farm

High Leases

Lownethwaite Farm

Low Leases

Belleisle

Callhall Wood

🅿 Round Howe Car Park

Caravan Park

Round Howe

Round Howe Wood

Billy Bank Wood

Richmond Bridge

Scotch Corner

Castle

RICHMOND

N

LEYBURN

THE CULLODEN TOWER

The Culloden Tower was built in honour of the Duke of Cumberland and to commemorate the defeat of the Scots at the Battle of Culloden in 1746. It has recently been restored and is now let out for holiday accommodation.

10   Willance's Leap and Round Howe

1 *(GR: 168 001)* From the car park entrance turn right and at the junction *(opposite the garage)* turn right again and continue along the main road.

2 *(GR: 167 011)* Turn right *(Westfields Road)* and follow the road uphill past the houses. Remain on the road to Whitcliffe Farm.

3 *(GR: 152 015)* Go past the farmhouse where the road surface reduces to a stone track. Follow the track to High Leases and pass through a gate. After a few yards cross a waymarked stile in the hedge on the right. Climb up to the top of the field and bear left along the line of a former hedgerow.

4 *(GR: 146 016)* Follow the track climbing to the top corner of the field, heading towards two aerial masts in the distance.

5 *(GR: 143 018)* Cross the double stile in the right corner of the field and follow the left fence through two fields. Go over two stiles and follow an enclosed path beside a small conifer plantation, cross another stile and proceed along the left fence.

6 *(GR: 136 021)* Go through the metal kissing gate to the Willance's Leap monuments. Turn right and proceed along the top of the scar. Continue round to the right and follow the wall to a cattle grid at the head of Deepdale.

7 *(GR: 129 019)* DO NOT CROSS THE CATTLE GRID, instead turn left and follow the narrow tarmac lane which descends into Deepdale.

8 *(GR: 128 019)* Before the cattle grid, leave the tarmac lane heading left to a gap stile *(SP Footpath this way)*. Turn left and descend alongside a ruined wall to a stile in the left wall *(SP Coast-to-Coast)*. DO NOT USE THIS STILE, instead go through a gap in the ruined wall and then descend steeply to a stile at the bottom of the field. Go through the stile and follow the left wall to an open gateway.

9 *(GR: 129 106)* Go through the gateway on the left and descend through three fields to reach the riverside. Continue downstream crossing two step stiles.

10 *(GR: 141 012)* The right of way bears left here towards Whitcliffe Wood BUT our route follows a 'permissive' path which continues along the riverside. Enter Whitcliffe Wood through a gate and follow a rough cart track climbing up gradually to Lownethwaite Farm.

11 *(GR: 148 009)* Go through a large metal gate on the left. Turn right and follow the right boundary which skirts round the farm. Cross a step stile and go through a gate onto the farm lane. Turn left and follow the lane to the main A6108 road.

12 *(GR: 155 009)* Turn left and follow the road, after about 30 yards (27m) cross the road and go through a gap in the wall opposite. Descend through the wood to reach the picnic area at Round Howe car park. Head left and pass through the car park to the entrance *(near the toilets)*. Cross the long footbridge over the river Swale.

13 *(GR: 157 008)* Go through a kissing gate, turn left and pass through another gate. Follow a tree-shaded track along the riverside. When the track divides take the right fork away from the river and go over a stile, continue through a gap in a hedge and then follow a broad green track.

14 *(GR: 164 008)* Before returning to the riverside, leave the track and go over a step stile into Billy Bank wood. Turn left and follow a clear path climbing up through the wood above the river, eventually leading back to the road at Richmond Bridge.

15 *(GR: 170 005)* Turn left and cross the bridge. At the green continue ahead onto Bridge Street and climb uphill. Follow New Road around the right bend and continue climbing to reach the market square. After visiting some of the attractions locate King Street and follow it to a roundabout. Turn left, follow the road to the garage, turn right onto Hurgill Road and then first left, returning to the Nuns' Close car park.

Information Desk

ABBEYS

Easby Abbey, near Richmond.
The substantial and interesting remains of this 12th century abbey are located close to the river Swale. It was founded by the one of the stricter monastic orders, the Premonstratensian Canons.

CASTLES

Richmond Castle, Richmond.
This mighty fortress was built by William the Conqueror in the 11th century to quell the rebellious North. Remains of the curtain wall and domestic buildings are combined with the 100 foot high keep added in the 12th century.

CRAFT CENTRES

Phillip Bastow, Cabinet Maker, Reeth.
Specialist in the design and manufacture of individual furniture commissions, using mainly oak, ash, elm and sycamore.

Joy Bentley Gallery, Reeth,
Paintings and sculpture, visiting artists, pottery, prints, silks, patchwork.

Pete Black, Guitar Maker, Reeth.
Showroom open to guitar enthusiasts with twenty plus guitars always on view or available to play.

Clock Works, Reeth.
Creators and constructors of fine clocks and barometers. Repairers and restorers of antique and contemporary clocks and barometers.

The Garden House, Reeth.
'Garden House' pottery, local patchwork and hand-knitting. Makers of 'Damson Cheese'.

Pots 'n' Presents, Reeth.
Cottage shop offering traditional handthrown stoneware pottery, silver jewellery and unusual gifts.

Old Schoolhouse Craft Shop & Gallery, Muker.
Serious sculpture, crafts, music.

Hazel Smith Gallery, Reeth.
Original paintings by Hazel and Vic Smith, showing the drama and beauty of the dales.

Shades of Heather, Reeth.
Traditional rug making - hooking, prodding and dyeing wools. Visitors by appointment.

Stef's Models, Reeth,
Animal figures and country wall plaques made from design stage to finished product.

Swaledale Woollens, Muker.
Unique cottage shop open all year round selling sweaters, cardigans, hats, scarves and gloves.

CYCLE HIRE

Dales Mountain Bike Hire, Fremington, Reeth.

H. S. Robinson, Kirby Stephen.

FARM VISITS

Hazel Brow Farm, Low Row.
Winner of Dales Environment award 1995. Farm visits and refreshments.

HISTORIC HOUSES

Aske Hall, Aske, Richmond.
The estate is at the gateway to the Yorkshire Dales on the outskirts of the ancient market town of Richmond. A Georgian coach house, with a clock tower housing the family's superb carriage which has recently been restored to its former splendour. There are also several follies including the Gothic style temple designed by Daniel Garret in 1745. The hall stands in Capability Brown landscaped parkland and overlooks a lake which serves as a natural wildlife sanctuary.

MUSEUMS

Georgian Theatre, Richmond.
A unique example of a Georgian Theatre with the majority of its original features intact. Built in 1788 by actor/manager Samuel Butler, it formed part of a theatre circuit which included Ripon, Harrogate, Beverley, Kendal, Ulverston and Whitby

Green Howards Regimental Museum, Richmond.
Set in a converted 12th century church, the museum's collection spans the 300 years of unbroken history of the Green Howards, one of Britain's oldest and most famous regiments.

Richmondshire Museum, Richmond.
This fascinating award winning museum presents the story of Richmondshire and its people. Transport in the Dales, a mediaeval cruck house, a James Heriot surgery set and local industry are featured.

Swaledale Folk Museum, Richmond.
The Swaledale Folk Museum depicts something of the way of life of the people of Swaledale, their farming implements, lead mining tools, pastimes and the impact of Wesleyan Methodism on their lives and thoughts.

OUTDOOR CENTRES

Marrick Priory Outdoor Education and Residential Centre, Marrick, Richmond.

Punch Bowl Leisure, Low Row.

RIDING & PONY TREKKING

Brookleigh Riding Centre, Eppleby, Richmond.

Arkle Moor Riding Centre, Arkengarthdale.

SWIMMING POOLS

Catterick, Catterick Garrison Camp Centre.

Richmond, Old Station Yard.

TOURIST INFORMATION POINTS

Barnard Castle, Woodleigh Flatts Road.

Kirby Stephen, 22 Market Street.

Reeth National Park Centre, The Green, Reeth.

Richmond, Friary Gardens, Queens Road.

Scotch Corner, Pavilion Service Area.

The Country Code

Enjoy the countryside and respect its life and works

Keep to public paths across farmland

Leave livestock, crops and farm machinery alone

Use gates and stiles to cross fences, hedges and walls

Guard against all risks of fire

Make no unnecessary noise

Fasten all gates

Take your litter home

Help to keep all water clean

Protect wildlife, plants and trees

Take special care on country roads

Keep your dogs under close control

Also . . .

Use car parks where possible and park with consideration for village residents and other road users.

Don't obstruct farm gates, tracks or entrances.

When walking on roads, walk on the right hand side to face oncoming traffic. When approaching blind bends, cross to the opposite side to enable you to see and be seen in both directions.

Allow sufficient time to complete the walk in daylight hours, and be sure to be off the fells by dusk.

Let people know the route you have taken, the time you expect to return and stick to the route.

If the weather turns nasty and you decide to quit the walk or take shelter in a hostelry etc., be sure to let others know so they don't worry and call out the emergency services unnecessarily.

Glossary

Many of the place names in Swaledale are Anglo-Saxon or Norse in origin. Anglo-Saxon names include those ending with *ing*, *ley*, *ham* and *ton*. Norse names include those ending with *by*, *sett* and *thwaite*. The Normans had a smaller influence on place names, being confined to changes in the spelling of existing names.

Aiskew: The oak wood.

Angram: The pastures.

Applegarth: Field with an apple tree.

Arkengarthdale: The valley of Arkil's enclosure.

Arkle Town: Arkil's farmstead.

Aygill: The river in a ravine.

Birkdale: The birch valley.

Blakethwaite: Dark clearing

Booze: The house on the curve of the hill.

Calver Hill: The hill where calves are pastured.

Calvert Houses: The calves' houses.

Catterick: The hillfort, or the waterfalls.

Cleasby: Kless's farmstead.

Clints: The rocky cliff.

Cogden: Woodcock valley.

Copperthwaite: The cooper's clearing.

Crackpot: The crevice where crows nest.

Cringley Hill: The curving hill.

Downholme: By the hills.

Easby: Esi's Farm

Ellers: The alders.

Ellerton: The farm near the alder tree.

Eskeleth: The hillside covered in ash trees.

Faggergill: The sheep fold in the ravine.

Feetham: The meadow.

Feldom: The open land.

Fremington: Frema's farm.

Grinton: The green enclosure.

Gunnerside: Gunnar's pasture.

Harkerside: Harker is an old local surname meaning to eavesdrop.

Healaugh: High forest clearing.

Helwith: The ford made of flat stones.

Hudswell: Hudel's well.

Hurst: The wooded hill.

Ivelet: Ifa's slope.

Keld: Spring or stream.

Kisdon: Small hill.

Kirby Hill: Church farm.

Kitley Hill: Hill near the cow valley.

Langthwaite: The long clearing.

Low Row: The low row of houses.

Marrick: The ridge where horses graze.

Marske: The marsh.

Melbecks Moor: The streams by the sandbank.

Muker: The small cultivated field.

Old Gang: The old road.

Owlands: Wolf grove.

Oxnop: The valley where the oxen are kept.

Rampsholme: The watermeadow where wild garlic grows.

Ravenseat: Hrafn's hilltop.

Ravensworth: Hrafn's ford.

Rawcroft: The rough pasture.

Raygill: The ravine.

Reeth: The place by the stream.

Richmond: The strong hill.

Riddings: The cleared land.

Satron: The wood cleared for pasture.

Shunner Fell: The look-out hill, or Sjon's mountain.

Skeb Sceugh: The wood where beehives are kept.

Skelton: The farm on a shelf of land.

Sleddale: The wide valley.

Smarber: The butter hill.

Storthwaite: The bullock clearing.

Stubbing: The place cleared of tree stumps.

Swale, River: The whirling, rushing river.

Swaledale: The valley of the Swale.

The Stang: The pole or stake.

Thwaite: (Arkil's) clearing.

Walburn: The foreigner's stream.

Whaw: The enclosure with a sheep fold.

Winterings: The meadows used for wintergrazing.